THE
CENTURY
OF
PRINT

BAUHAUSBÜCHER

EDITORS:
WALTER GROPIUS
L. MOHOLY-NAGY

A BAUHAUS EXPERIMENTAL HOUSE IN WEIMAR

3

A BAUHAUS EXPERIMENTAL HOUSE IN WEIMAR

COMPILED BY
ADOLF MEYER

LARS MÜLLER PUBLISHERS

THE EXPERIMENTAL HOUSE WAS BUILT FOR THE FIRST PUBLIC BAUHAUS EXHIBITION (SUMMER 1923) IN WEIMAR AM HORN

BY GEORG MUCHE (DRAFT) AND THE ARCHITECTURE DEPARTMENT OF THE BAUHAUS

CONSTRUCTION ADOLF MEYER / WALTER MARCH

This book was produced in summer 1924. Technical difficulties prevented its timely publication. The individuals who constituted the former State Bauhaus have completed their activities in Weimar and continue as

DAS BAUHAUS IN DESSAU (ANHALT).

Originally published in German by Albert Langen Verlag München in 1924, printed by Dietsch & Brückner A.-G. Weimar, printing blocks by Bruckmann A.-G. München.
First English edition published by Lars Müller, based on the first German edition.
Translation by Helen Ferguson.

ISBN 978-3-03778-627-7
Printed in Germany
www.lars-mueller-publishers.com

FITTINGS AND INTERIOR DESIGN: IN COOPERATION WITH GERMAN INDUSTRY, THE COMPANY ADOLF SOMMERFELD, BERLIN AND THE WORKSHOPS OF THE STATE BAUHAUS

PRINTING: DZA DRUCKEREI ZU ALTENBURG
REPRODUCTION: INTEGRAL LARS MÜLLER
TYPOGRAPHY: ADOLF MEYER, WEIMAR

WALTER GROPIUS

5

HOUSING INDUSTRY

Man is indubitably capable of constructing his home adequately and well, but his own inner sluggishness and sentimental attachment to the past have so far prevented him from doing so in practice. The harshness of contemporary world events forces states and individuals to overcome this inertia. By adjusting to changed global conditions, it finally becomes possible to realize the old idea of building typical dwellings more cheaply, better and in greater numbers than ever before and creating a healthy foundation for every family. Generally viable solutions that truly suit modern times have not yet been developed, because the problem of housing construction itself has not yet been grasped anywhere in its full sociological, economic, technical and formal structure and subsequently solved systematically and on a large scale from scratch. So far, people have always remained mired in tendentious minor problems, questions of substitute materials and cost-cutting measures, in considerations pertaining to cultivation of the land or to aesthetics. Once the full scope of intellectual requirements impinging on the housing problem has however been clearly identified and outlined, tactical implementation will only be a question of methodology and large-scale organization.

This master plan, this "how do we want to live?" as the generally applicable fruit of reflections that draw on the present's spiritual and material possibilities, does not yet exist. Residential housing's chaotic heterogeneity demonstrates that that our notions of the right dwelling, fitting for modern individuals, remain highly unclear.

Does it, for example, really reflect human lifestyles that each individual's dwelling is entirely different from all the others? Is it not a sign of intellectual impoverishment and flawed thinking to furnish one's home in Rococo or Renaissance style, whilst humans all over the world wear the same modern apparel? Advances in technology over the last three generations outstrip those attained over millennia before us. Confident in this state of affairs, let us resolve to make bold demands, so that the spirit may become freer and freer thanks to organization of all material work. Perhaps mobile vessels for living, which would allow us to take all the ease of genuinely comfortable living with us even every time we moved to a different location, are no longer merely a distant utopia.

6 Human accommodation is an issue of mass demand. Just as today it no longer occurs to 90 percent of the population to have their footwear made to measure, for instead they buy off-the-shelf products that satisfy most individual needs, thanks to fine-tuned manufacturing methods, in future each individual will also be able to order the dwelling best suited to him direct from the warehouse. Today's technology might already be sufficiently mature to enable this, but today's construction industry is still tied almost entirely to old artisanal construction methods; the machine plays only a minor role in this context. Radical transformation of the entire construction industry to adopt a more industrial approach is therefore urgently needed in order to find a contemporary solution to this important problem. This must be tackled simultaneously from three different angles, addressing economic-organizational, technical and formal issues; all three are directly interdependent. Satisfactory solutions can only be found by simultaneously addressing all three areas, as a single individual cannot get to grips with this profusion of questions; only a concerted strategy cooperating with numerous experts can do so.

Reducing the price of housing is of crucial importance for the national budget. Attempts to reduce the cost of traditional craftsmanship deployed to date by streamlining operating methods have brought only limited progress. The problem was not tackled at its root. The new goal, on the other hand, would be factory-scale mass production of turn-key residential houses that must no longer be built on the construction site but are made in special factories as individual components ready for assembly. The advantages of this production method would be all the greater to the extent that components pre-fabricated in factories could be assembled at the construction site like machines using dry construction methods. Such dry assembly-based construction, to be elucidated in greater detail, would eliminate the troublesome alteration of building components caused by moisture within the construction, and would do away with time-wasted drying out for houses built with masonry mortar and plaster according to traditional bricks-and-mortar construction methods. This would make construction independent of the weather and season in one fell swoop.

This kind of industrial construction process is only conceivable on a broad financial basis. Small individual contractors, engineers or architects will never be able to implement these building techniques on their own. The general contractor format, on the other hand, which encompasses all the various branches, has proved its economic viability in other fields too. Many building clients would therefore first have to realize this, before consumer organizations and vertical companies could be formed with sufficient financial strength to ensure the implementation of such large-scale processes. The economic advantages of this construction method would certainly be enormous. Experienced experts estimate that savings of 50 percent or more could be expected. This would signify that every working person would have an opportunity to obtain a good, healthy home for his family, just as today he can buy daily necessities more cheaply than previous generations could thanks to the development of world industry. Lower prices for these products came about due to increasing use of mechanical power – steam and electricity – rather than manual labor; reducing the price of house construction will also entail making use of these forces.

The other significant cost-reducting option lies in a new, farsighted financial policy that deliberately avoids the higher interest rates on building capital caused by unproductive intermediaries in financial transactions.

Before decisive preparatory organizational work can come into play to solve the industrial mass production problem, the question of housing needs must be sufficiently clarified to allow generally valid, concise requirements to be articulated: "How do we want to live?" As a consequence, numerous habits will prove superfluous and outdated, e.g. it will be possible to reduce the size of rooms in order to increase living comfort. Most people in civilized nations have similar requirements for their housing and living situation. That makes it impossible to understand why the dwellings we build do not share the uniform precision of our clothes, shoes, suitcases, automobiles. There is just as little reason to fear the undesirable coercion of individual needs due to such uniformity as there is to fear the impact of fashion. There is no justification for every house in a suburban development having a different ground plan, a different exterior, a different architectural style and different building materials; on the contrary, this state of affairs means senseless waste and signals a parvenu lack of culture. The old farmhouse in the north and south, the 18th-century burgher's townhouse, for example, had a consistent, almost uniform design in their floor plans and overall design throughout all European countries. The threat of complete uniformization, however, as in the English suburban house, for example, must be tackled, for suppressing individuality is always short-sighted and erroneous. The proper organization must intervene and do the groundwork for planning the house building in such a way that justified individual needs, arising from the number of occupants or their professions, can be fulfilled appropriately. As a result, the organization must aim to ensure that it is not first and foremost entire

STANDARDIZED MASS-PRODUCED HOUSE BY WALTER GROPIUS

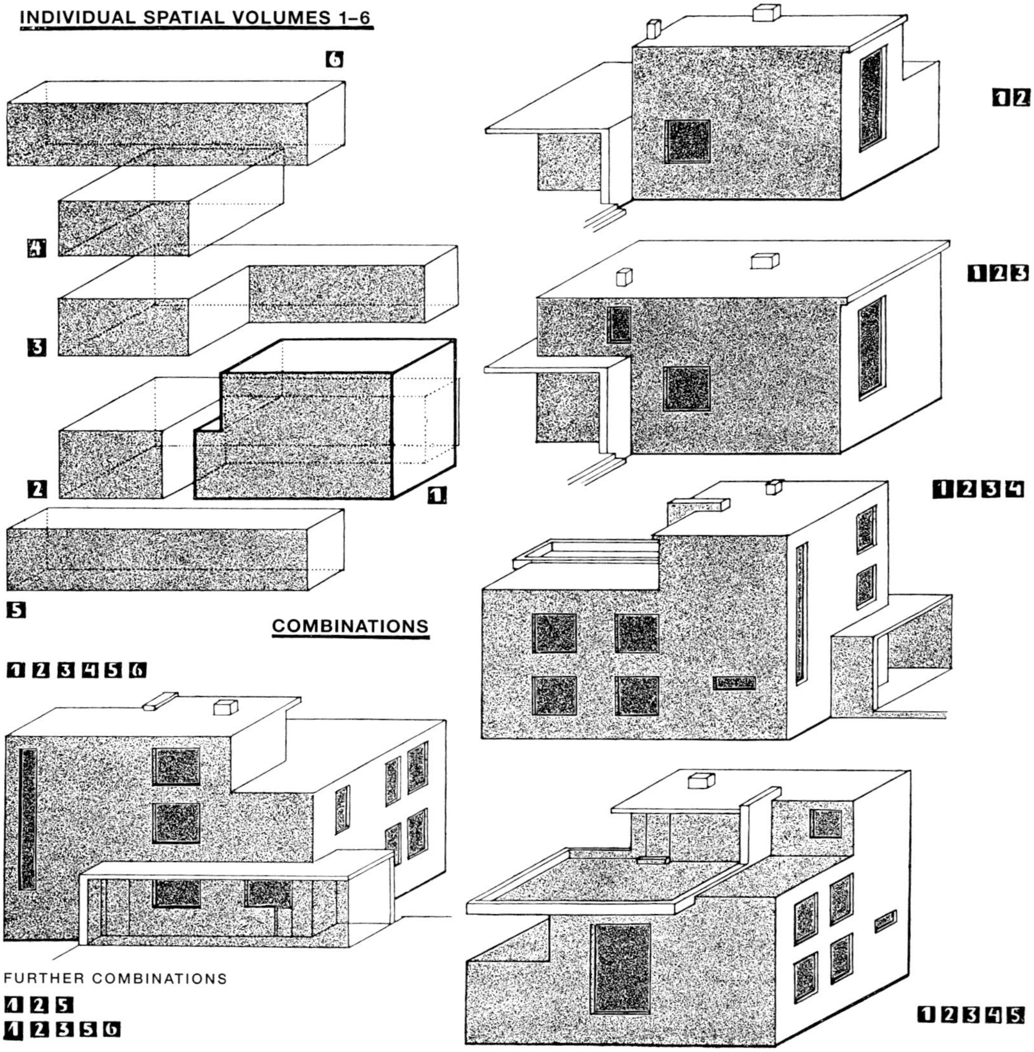

LARGE-SCALE CONSTRUCTION KIT, FROM WHICH VARIOUS "MACHINES FOR LIVING" CAN BE ASSEMBLED ACCORDING TO PREPARED ASSEMBLY PLANS, DEPENDING ON THE NUMBER AND NEEDS OF THE RESIDENTS

houses that are standardized and industrially produced, but rather their components, which can then be assembled into various types of houses, just as certain standardized parts are used internationally in various machines in mechanical engineering today. Planning for "off-the-peg" availability entails the production of all individual construction components in various special factories, so that these could be ordered as required at the construction site, as well as field-tested assembly plans for various types of houses in a range of sizes. Since all standardized and mass-produced machine-made parts fit together perfectly, the building can be rapidly assembled at the construction site, with minimum labor, partly with unskilled workers, at any time of the year and regardless of the weather, thanks to precise assembly plans. Above all, however, the numerous embarrassing surprises and chance occurrences that were unavoidable consequences of the old construction method can now finally be avoided: ill-fitting installation parts due to imprecise wall dimensions or dampness in the plaster, unforeseen day labor, loss of time and interest payments due to delayed drying, as well as the consequences of generally over-hasty planning of custom-made designs for houses. Instead: absolutely precise fit of the machined components, fixed price and short, clearly stipulated construction time guaranteed.

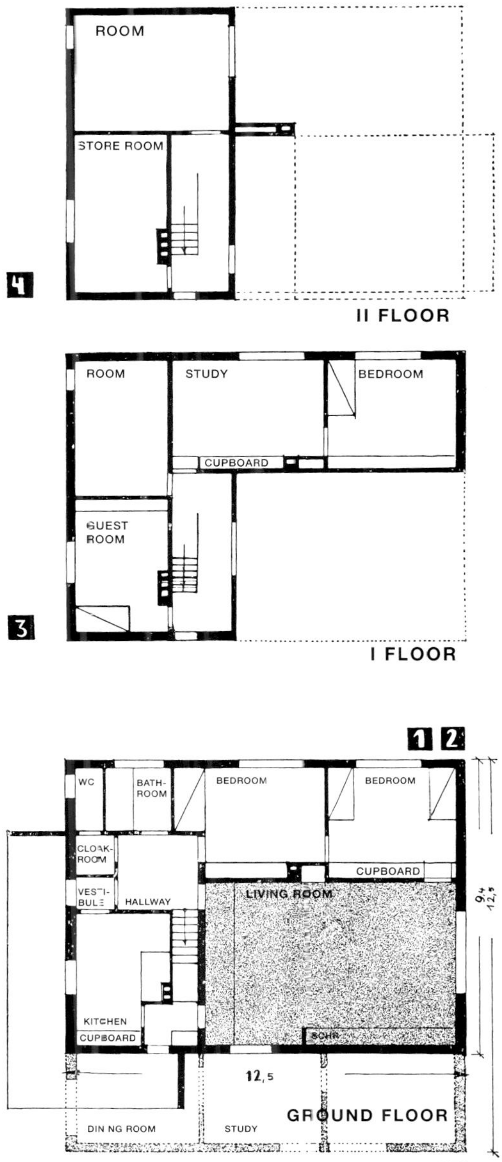

VARIABLE FLOOR PLAN
OF THE SERIES HOUSES P. 6

Implementing this economic-organizational scheme is in the first task a matter for the engineers. In their field, too, this problem is a radical revolution compared with previous developments in construction technology, whether one thinks of the building materials or of structural design. Most buildings today are constructed with the help of the old natural building materials: stone, brick and wood. The house is mainly built at the construction site. All the auxiliary equipment and machinery must be brought to the construction site for this purpose, clogging up the traffic. One drawback of these mobile plants compared with stationary factories is that they can only be primitive. Constructing the shell of the building using conventional methods affords no scope to calculate in advance how long the structural work will take to dry or the time needed to complete the interior, for both depend on the weather. Technically perfecting this conventional construction method, for example by using larger building blocks or more uniform and rational organization of building work at the construction site, did not, however, result in any significant simplification or lower costs. In order to tap into the advantages of dry-assembly construction, different building materials will therefore have to be used now, machine-processed instead of natural, unprocessed material. The aim here would not be to create substitute materials, but rather to improve natural, products so that they become absolutely reliable, precisely uniform materials (rolled steel, cement alloys, synthetic wood). A standardized solution to the problem will only be possible if all parts required for house construction, including walls, ceilings and roofs, are industrially produced.

MODEL FOR SERIAL HOUSE P. 8 (1. 2. 3. 4.)

To this end, the houses' structural design must also undergo a fundamental change. Either a more lightweight, less voluminous material must be found to replace the load-bearing, insulating capacity of conventional

MODEL FOR SERIAL HOUSE P. 8 (1. 2. 3. 4.)

solid masonry, allowing this material to be positioned in large story-height sections, or the building must be divided into a structural skeleton (iron, reinforced concrete) and non-load-bearing components fitted into it i.e. walls, roofs and ceilings. This kind of structural skeleton can be made of iron beams and columns or reinforced concrete beams and pillars, connected to each other in a cantilever or rigid frame system, similar to the load-bearing timbers in half-timbered buildings. The infill elements of the walls, ceilings and roofs will consist of standardized construction slabs, which must be mechanically produced from weather-resistant, structurally stable, porous, insulating, tough lightweight material. Initial steps towards developing such building panels can already be seen in conventional pumice cement and gypsum planks and in reinforced Torfoleum building panels. An appropriate solution is still needed for industrial production of the wall, ceiling and roof segments and for the right structural skeleton. Standardization and mass production of doors, windows, stairs, cornices, fixtures and interior fittings, on the other hand, is already being fine-tuned, although it is still based on manual labor more than on industrial mass production. Vehicle engineers who develop railroad cars, ships, automobiles and planes have the edge on building engineers when it comes to building methods and materials, for vehicle engineers have already begun to work with machine-processed, homogeneous construction materials (iron, aluminum, glass) and mechanized manufacturing processes for components made from these materials. Their experiences therefore have direct relevance for mass housing construction.

The new construction method should also be welcomed from an artistic point of view. It is completely erroneous to assume that turning house construction into an industrialized process would give rise to ugly building forms. On the contrary,

12

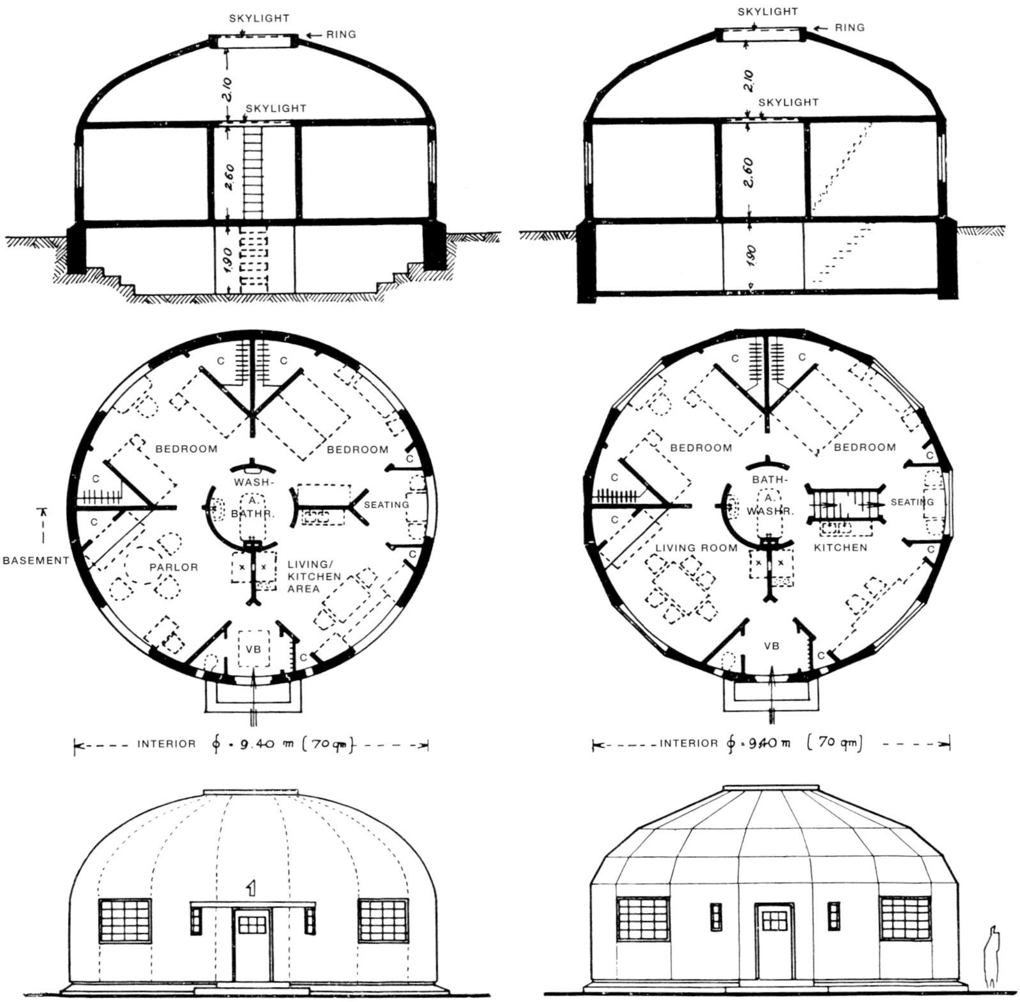

A ROUNDHOUSE BY KARL FIEGER

Goal: A homogeneous building material processed in factories, therefore saving on construction workers, the mathematically most economical use of space (circular dome).

Design: 16 standardized self-supporting lightweight panels with the most efficient structural connection, joined together by a "skylight ring." Upright wall that fits together with the roofing. Carpentry, roofing, plumbing work are no longer required. Lightweight panels made of porous, load-bearing lightweight material, insulating against heat and cold, smoothed on the interior, coated with a waterproof layer on the exterior. (Saving on external and internal plasterwork.) At ceiling height, brackets for fixing together the wall panels, which also support the false ceiling. – The parts cut to shape in series from lightweight panels, the partition walls and false ceilings, the standardized floor panels, doors and windows, make specialized workmen on site superfluous and can be assembled by a fitter. A rainwater gutter is provided in the foundation ring. – A second form of execution: a strong iron or aluminum skeleton. The dome is infilled with the help of the shotcrete process using concrete door and window frames.

standardizing building elements will have the salutary effect of ensuring the new residential buildings and districts share a common character. There is no reason to fear they will be monotonous, as for example English suburban houses are, provided that one basic requirement is fulfilled: only construction components will be standardized, whereas the buildings erected with these components, on the other hand, will vary. In manufacturing standardized components, the decisive parameters for their organic design will be their intended purpose and function. Well-processed material and clear, simple construction will guarantee their "beauty," not aesthetic ornamental forms and profiles that are simply added on rather than being determined by the building methods and material. The extent to which these building elements, this "large-scale construction kit," gives rise to well-designed space in the building depends on the architect's creative talent. In any case, standardization of components does not impose limits on the individual design that we all desire, and the reappearance of individual parts and the same materials in various structures will create an impression of order and calm, in the same way as uniform clothing does. In precisely the same way, sufficient scope remains for the unique character of the individual and the nation to have an impact, but then everything is imbued with the character of our era.

The extensive problem of putting housing construction on an industrial footing can only be solved by deploying exceptional public resources. It is so important from an economic point of view that lay people and experts must urge the state to make public preparations to attain a solution. As the largest building clients, states and municipalities have an economic and cultural obligation to use every means available to bring about a reduction in the cost of housing. The approach adopted to date, involving promotion of substitutes and savings-oriented building methods, as advocated by the Reich after the war, did not lead to the desired result. Public experimental construction sites must be set up! Just as the form of an object to be mass produced stems from countless experiments systematically conducted in a preliminary phase, which must involve salespeople, technicians and artists on an equal footing, before the typified form, the standard, is determined, production of standardized construction components can be achieved only through a broadminded alliance between the worlds of industry, business and the arts. This would signify true foresight and thrift, not the creation of "substitute construction methods." It is clear that the first model houses require significant resources, as did the prototypes developed in industry's experimental laboratories, which served as the basis for cheaper mass production. Financing this kind of experimentation is a matter for consumer organizations, which will benefit from cheaper buildings subsequently. They are therefore first and foremost interested in establishing excellent test sites, where, in keeping with a consistent management concept, the achievements to date can be outlined in a plan and tested with a view to the new construction method. Such a profound change in the construction industry will, of course, take place only gradually. However, despite all objections it will ineluctably occur; for no argument can justify the tremendous waste of resources, time and labor that arises from continued construction of housing estates and residential ensembles according to countless individual designs, all different, using manual labor, rather than using mass construction methods based on standardized plans.

MODELS FOR SERIAL HOUSES. VARIABILITY OF THE SAME BASIC TYPE BY ALTERNATELY ADDING ROOM CELLS ADJACENT TO AND ABOVE EXISTING CELLS.

GEORG MUCHE

THE BAUHAUS EXPERIMENTAL HOUSE

The most beautiful houses are of no use if their inhabitants do not adopt the achievements of modern times in their lifestyles as well.

Old-fashioned attitudes turn even the most beautiful and practical house into a junk room crammed with impractical, outdated furniture, with superfluous handicrafts, with memories and heirlooms, or into a house museum, aspiring to express its inhabitants' particularly good taste through an accumulation of art and objects from various stylistic epochs of bygone craft traditions.

Such houses do not belong in the present day. They document the past to a much greater degree than is good for progressive urban development and hygiene.

The ideal of the house lies in the future and not in any past cultural epochs. It arises from the cultural, social, economic and hygienic demands of our times. The dwelling is an amenity to nurture humans' physical and mental health. It must be fine-tuned hand-in-hand with scientific research and technological inventions. By applying the principles of the greatest expediency and economy and replacing human labor by mechanical and electrical power as much as possible, the household must be transformed, perfected and simplified.

The inconvenience and impracticality of conventional household management is a threat that often virtually destroys family life. The woman of the house is degraded to mere labor power by having banal, mechanical labor heaped upon her. She becomes indifferent to the higher tasks of life and thus tends to seek her ideals sentimentally in the past. She contributes, without ever having intending to, to the atrophying of family life, which ceases to be a place to nurture and develop the aspirations of the age.

Mistakenly furnishing the kitchen as if it were just another room is the cause of many difficulties and proves exceedingly time-consuming. The kitchen should be the housewife's workplace, her laboratory, in which any superfluous dimensions and unwieldy arrangement of fittings constantly causes extra work. The kitchen must become a mechanism, an instrument. Time should be too precious for the woman of the house to have to bear the drudgery of old-fashioned kitchen management day in, day out.

Until women can be freed from these burdens by eliminating individual housekeeping through the introduction of the large cooperative house, efforts must be made to constantly improve the spatial arrangement and economic organization of individual housing. The cooperative house, in which each individual and each family can rent the number and type of rooms required (unfurnished or furnished, with or without kitchen), with housekeeping and running of the house conducted according to the residents' wishes by a specially trained group of workers, corresponds exceedingly closely to the structure of today's economic life.

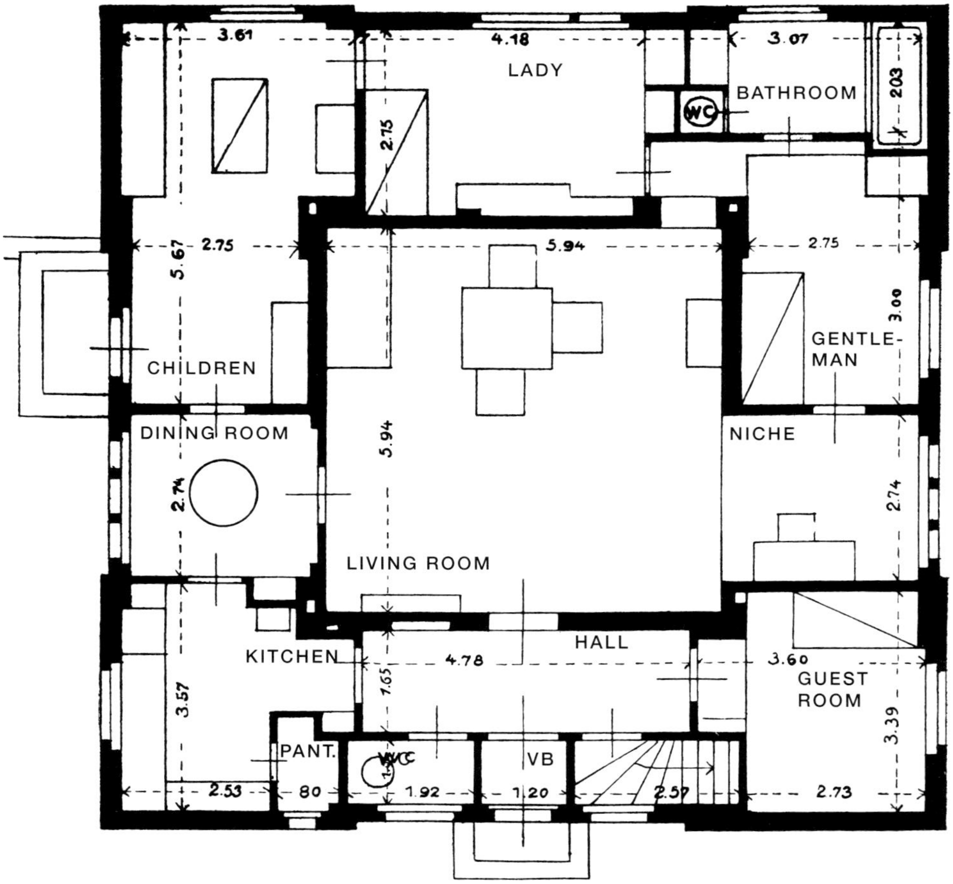

FLOOR PLAN **DESIGN: GEORG MUCHE**

The apartment's formal design must embody the sense of style of the world today. The spirit informing the design language of furnishings and fittings should tally with the possibilities afforded by industrialized and standardized mechanized work, for there is no risk that our times will become depleted of beauty and descend into barbaric formlessness if mechanical working methods are deployed in formal design contexts too.

Modern design for houses and flats is a prerequisite for and an object of urban modernization, a wider reach for the state's activities, improved living conditions and realization of the people's cultural possibilities.

For its exhibition in summer 1923, the State Bauhaus built a single-family house, with an interior layout that represents an attempt to determine the contemporary detached house's basic design. In this first house, a schematic floor plan layout was deliberately chosen (extra-high large central living space with smaller and lower adjoining rooms distributed rhythmically around it). This arrangement proves practical, making it possible to make the house relatively small and thus simultaneously cut costs, both for construction and for running the household. Too many rooms, particularly if these are large, make constant extra work for the residents.

The 12.70 × 12.70 m floor plan is structured to establish a functional relationship between the individual rooms. Corridors and stairs were therefore made constrainted as much as possible or avoided entirely. The individual rooms were furnished according to their purpose. The kitchen should be purely a kitchen and not a common room for the family (i.e. not a combined kitchen/living room). It is practically equipped with all labor-saving amenities: water heater, kitchen sink, bucket sink, exterior and in-house telephone lines, plug contact for electric power, gas and electric stove, pantry, broom and bucket cupboard. The table stands in front of the window and forms a wide, continuous work surface, all at the same height, together with the stove, the tops of the low crockery cupboards and the kitchen sink; this small room has as much usable surface area as a conventional kitchen two to three times its size.

The pantry and storerooms, the laundry room (with electrically operated washing machine and drier) and the boiler of the central heating system were accommodated in the bright basement rooms.

The dining room should only be a dining room and not a study and living room at the same time. It is only equipped for people to spend relatively short periods there and must therefore simply accommodate six to eight people seated comfortably at the table. The crockery cupboard is built in, so that this room contains only the

2

MAIN FACADE SEEN FROM THE STREET AM HORN WITH MAIN ENTRANCE

furniture absolutely necessary for a dining room, with a floor divided into color sections with colorfully finished walls and an elevated, wide window. It is not fitted out with rugs or the usual sideboard. At the same time, the position of the dining room protects the other rooms of the house from cooking smells. On the side facing the corridor, the kitchen is also insulated by an entryway. In contrast to the other rooms, the central living room, where the residents spend most of their time, is as large as possible. The surrounding rooms protect the large room (6×6 m) from cooling down due to the outside temperature, and as the ceiling and the outside walls, as well as the extra-high wall areas of this room are insulated by Torfoleum, this part of the house is also easy to heat and is well protected against the warmth of the sun in summer. Light enters the interior space through elevated side windows (double glass with inner frosted glass pane) and through a wide window in the desk niche.

The parents' bedroom has plentiful built-in closet space and is furnished as a double room with an en-suite bathroom and laundry room. For practical and aesthetic reasons, the bathroom walls are covered with white alabaster glass. Rubber was used as floor covering.

The children's room has direct access to the lady's bedroom and a door to the terrace. It has been equipped to create the most opportune, healthy environment possible for the children. Yellow, blue and red writing boards extend about halfway up the walls. The play closet is partly composed of easily adjustable, light-colored boxes that can be used equally well for children's chairs and tables, for building blocks and for playing. The rest of the room is equipped with a linen chest, bed and washbasin with running water. – Using fluorescent lamps as room lighting is a new experiment. The formal design of the sockets and tubes with partial matting or a reflective coating make the use of a special luminaire superfluous. By deftly combining several tubes, the whole lighting system creates a beautiful effect.

SECTION
VIEW
FLOOR PLAN

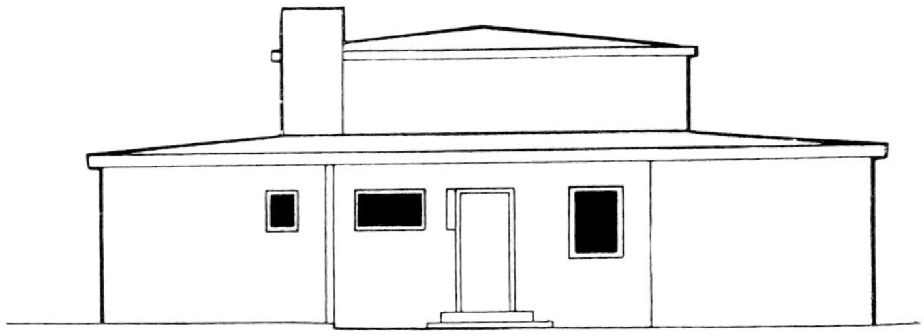

ENTRANCE SIDE

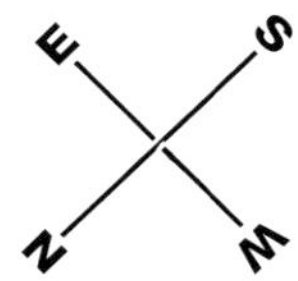

HEIGHT OF TERRAIN

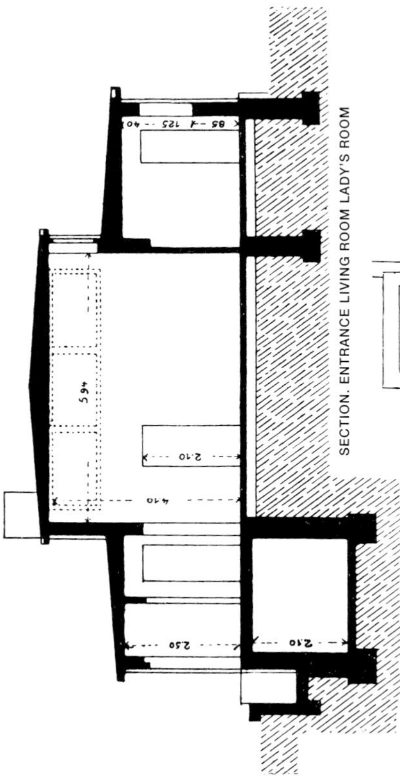

SECTION. ENTRANCE LIVING ROOM LADY'S ROOM

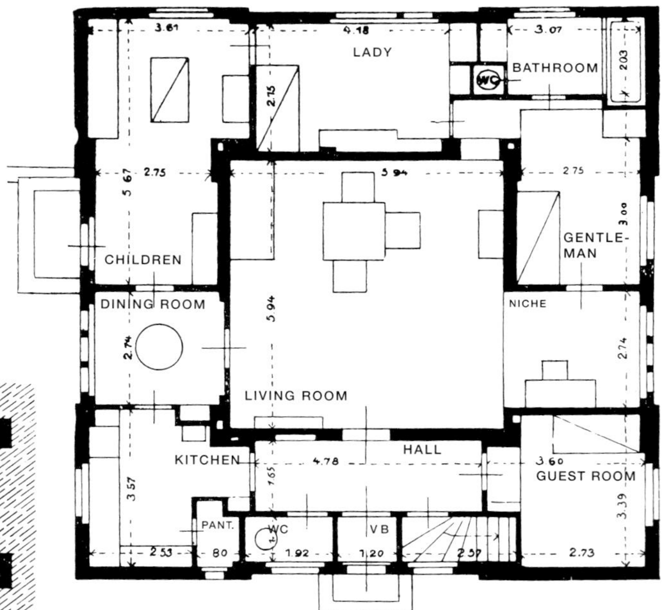

FLOOR PLAN.

SITE PLAN WITH GARDEN

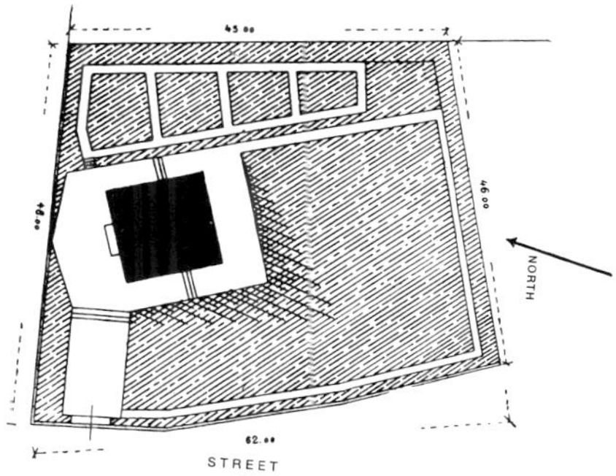

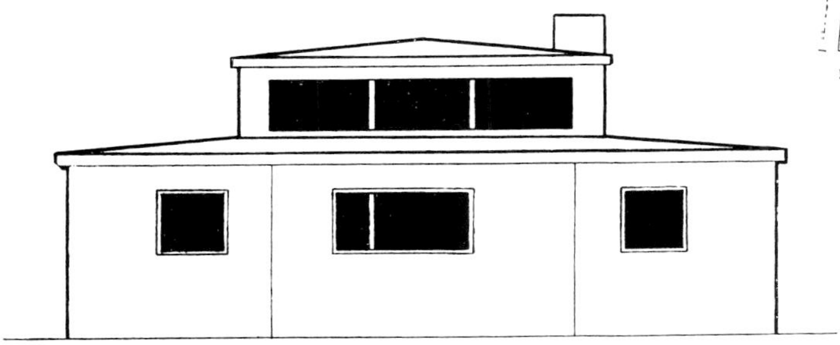

SOUTH-EAST SIDE

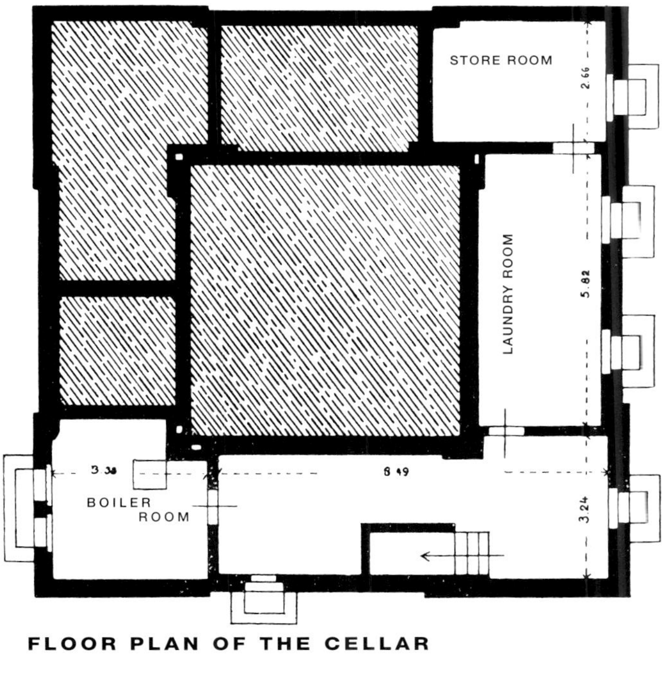

FLOOR PLAN OF THE CELLAR

NORTH-EAST SIDE

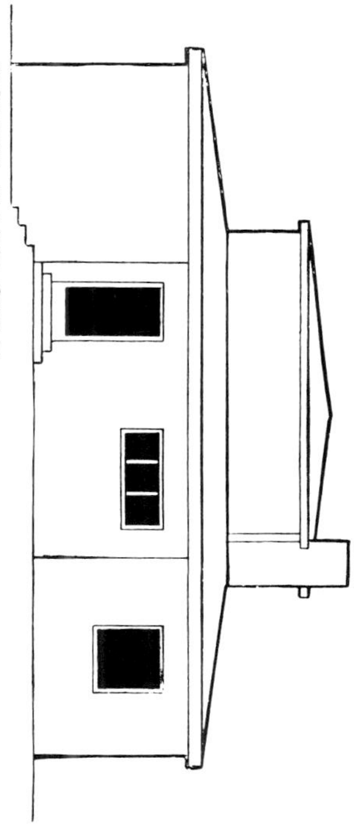

VARIATIONS

THE DESIGNS ON PAGES 22 AND 23 ARE VARIANTS OF THE EXPERIMENTAL HOUSE. THEY DEMONSTRATE THE ADAPTABILITY OF THIS TYPOLOGY.

TYPE 2

SINGLE FAMILY HOUSE WITH HIGH-CEILINGED LIVING ROOM, SURROUNDING ROOMS ON THREE SIDES. ADOLF MEYER

TYPE 3

SINGLE FAMILY HOUSE WITH HIGH-CEILINGED LIVING ROOM, SURROUNDING ROOMS ON TWO SIDES. MARCEL BREUER

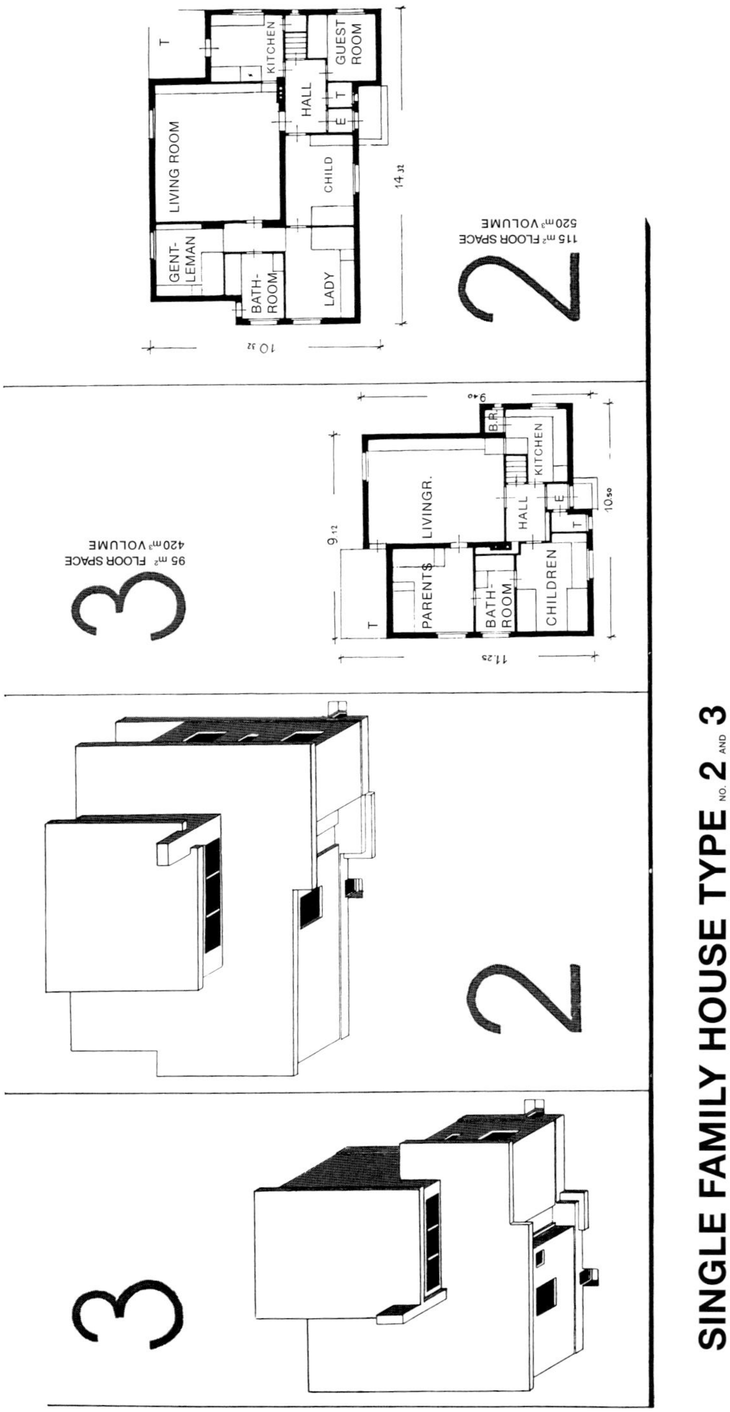

TERRACED HOUSE WITH HIGH-CEILINGED LIVING ROOM

W. MOLNAR

142 m^2 FLOOR SPACE
540 m^3 VOLUME

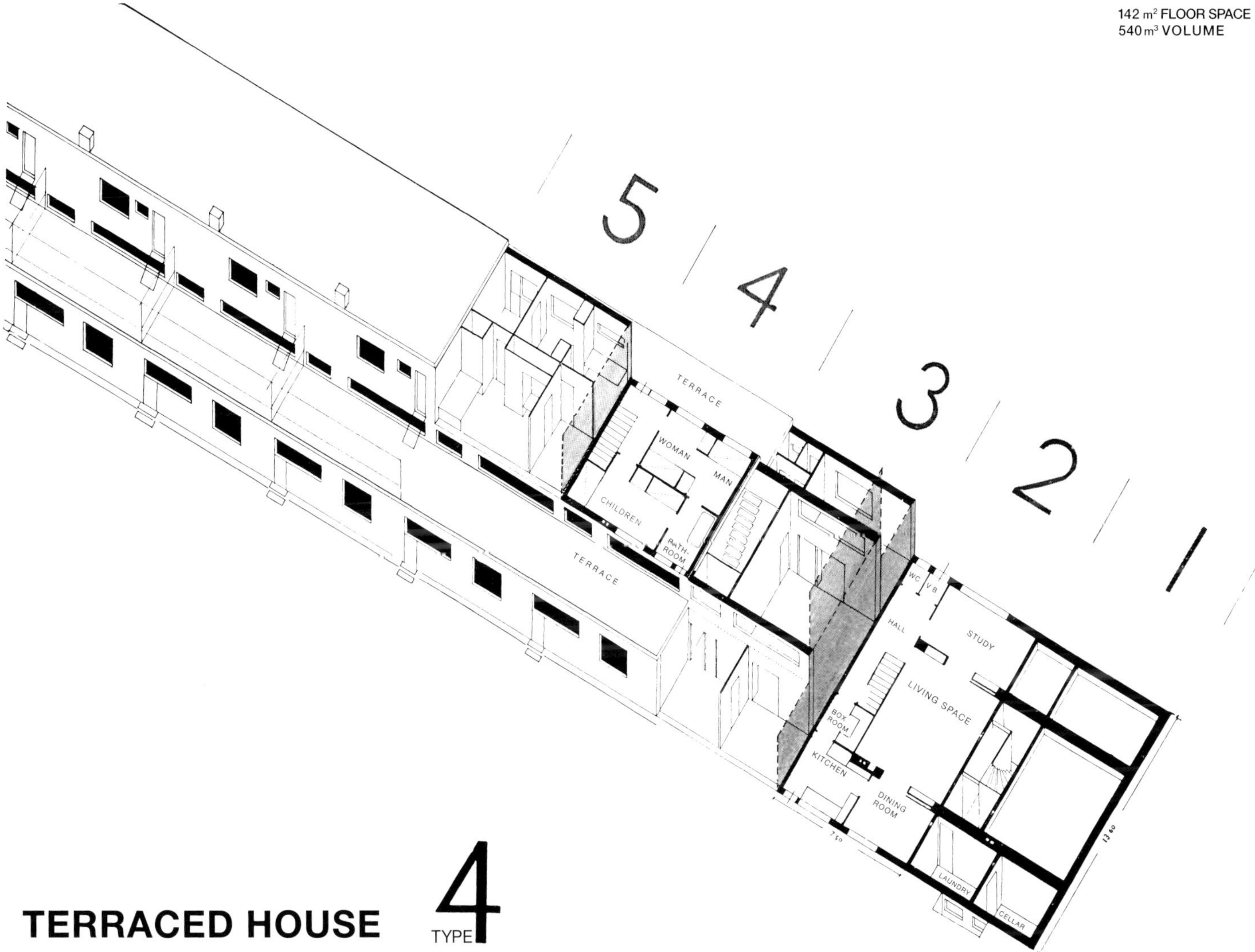

TERRACED HOUSE TYPE 4

ADOLF MEYER

STRUCTURAL DESIGN OF THE EXPERIMENTAL HOUSE

The State Bauhaus single family home was built in 1923 as the first house in a planned estate.

The construction period lasted four months. The foundation stone was laid on April 11 and the building was completed on August 15, 1923.

The construction period coincided with the period of inflation. There were therefore certain constraints on the choice of building materials and the structural design. It was essentially thanks to the understanding and cooperation of the industrial firms involved that a building could be constructed in keeping with today's building technology.

When selecting building materials and structural designs, preference was given to those in tune with a new, synthetic approach to building.

Construction methods based on the use of substitute materials were deliberately excluded; in contrast, the emphasis was placed on ensuring a correspondence between material and structural design to demonstrate a way forward that is already possible today, despite current economic constraints. This overview of the building makes it possible to determine to what extent this has already been achieved.

The following pages list the industries and trades that participated in the construction work according to the sequence in which they were involved. Illustrations of the most important work processes in the building are included with a presentation and description of the construction methods and materials. – The other photographs show the finished individual parts being installed on site, and offer a general impression of the interiors. An attempt has thus been made to offer a cross-section through the building's entire genesis.

These photographs are carefully arranged to help readers gain an overview, an organic overall impression and an understanding of the new problems facing construction.

TECHNICAL EXECUTION

A SKELETON CONSTRUCTION WORK
B FINISHING WORK
C INSTALLATION WORK
D INTERIOR DESIGN

A SKELETON CONSTRUCTION WORK

CEMENT

THE MOST IMPORTANT BUILDING MATERIAL TODAY.

USED: AS A COMPONENT AND CONNECTING ELEMENT FOR MOST STRUCTURAL WORK FROM THE BASE OF THE FOUNDATIONS TO THE CHIMNEY COVERS. COMPONENT IN JURKO BLOCKS, SYNTHETIC STONEWORK, EXTERIOR AND INTERIOR PLASTERING (TERRANOVA) AND ASBESTOS SLABS

CEMENT SUPPLIED BY:
DEUTSCHER ZEMENTBUND G.M.B.H. THROUGH SÄCHS.-THÜR. PORTLAND-ZEMENT-FABRIK PRÜSSING & CO. KOMMANDIT-GES. AUF AKTIEN, GÖSCHWITZ A. D. S.

JURKO BLOCKS LARGE-FORMAT STANDARDIZED PANELS

FAST BUILDING • FAST DRYING • INSULATING AIR LAYERS • BREATHABLE WALLS • HEAT-RETAINING • SOUND-DAMPING • LIGHT WEIGHT • LITTLE MORTAR REQUIRED

SAVINGS COMPARED TO BRICK MASONRY WALLS:

IN COAL ——— BECAUSE NOT FIRED
IN MORTAR ——— BECAUSE OF FEW MORTAR JOINTS
IN TRANSPORT COSTS ——— BECAUSE OF LOW NET WEIGHT
IN BUILT AREA ——— BECAUSE OF LOW WALL THICKNESS
IN WAGES ——— BECAUSE OF LARGE FORMAT

SKELETON PHOTOGRAPH: WALL CONSTRUCTION WITH JURKO PANELS

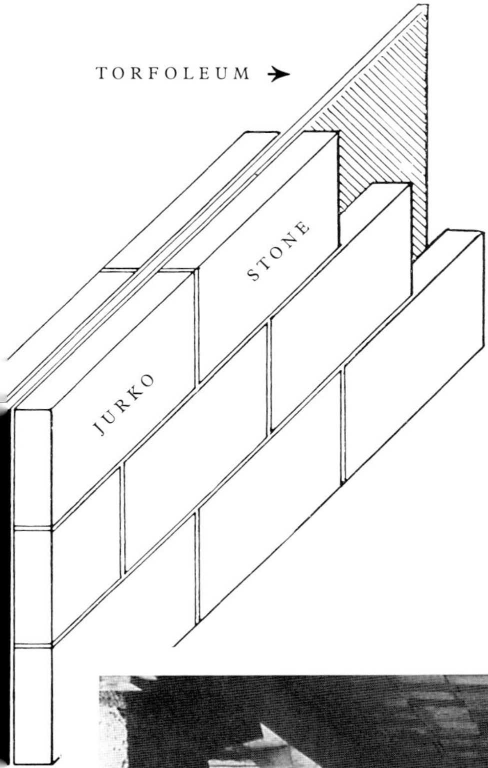

JURKO STANDARDIZED PANELS USED IN EXPERIMENTAL CONSTRUCTION WITH CONTINUOUS TORFOLEUM INSULATION BETWEEN THE PANELS

FORMAT:

54•32•10cm and 32•26•8cm

MATERIAL:

SLAG CONCRETE
PUMICE-STONE
PUMICE
OR SIMILAR
MATERIAL MIXED
WITH CEMENT

SKELETON PHOTOGRAPH INTERIOR BY THE MAIN ENTRANCE

28 JURKO BLOCKS SUPPLIED BY:

VERBAND SOZIALER BAUBETRIEBE G.M.B.H.
BERLIN THROUGH WERK NORDHAUSEN

EXECUTION OF ALL STRUCTURAL WORK:
SOZIALE BAUHÜTTE WEIMAR

NEW USE OF JURKO BLOCKS AS CELLAR CEILING
BY ARCHITECT EMIL LANGE • WEIMAR-BRESLAU

SMOKE AND VENTILATION CHIMNEYS

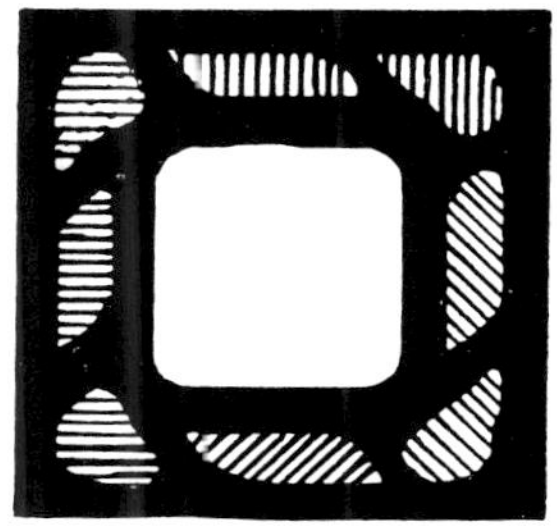

SCHOFERS

COMPOUND SMOKE AND VENTILATION CHIMNEYS:
DAMPFZIEGELEI AKTIEN-GESELLSCHAFT WAIBLINGEN

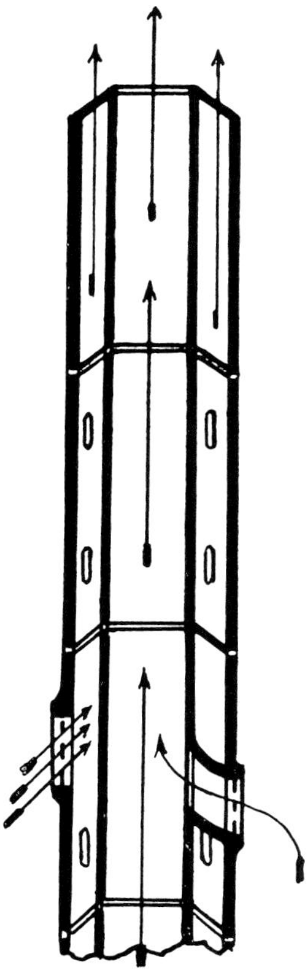

Material: steel-reinforced brick ballast concrete, high-stability fire brick with good fire safety properties, light weight
excellent ventilation opportunity through the insulation shafts surrounding the smoke duct
making special ventilation ducts superfluous
absolute fire safety, because the standardized parts are large format, therefore few joints, every 70 cm
no draught loss, no smoke nuisance, excellent draughting, because the smoke duct is surrounded by air insulation shafts, whereby cooling of the smoke duct is avoided.
Easy to install.
Space saving.
Application: Main smoke duct for the central heating system, ventilation of all living space, the bathroom, the toilet and the cellars through the ventilation ducts

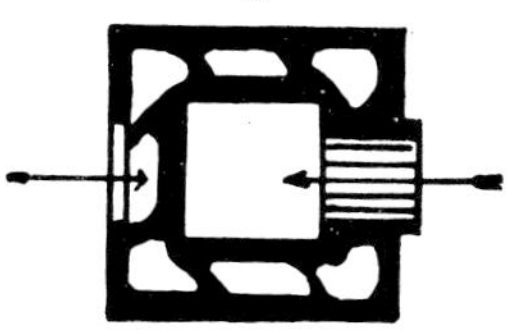

SCHEMATIC DRAWING OF THE CHIMNEY

HOLLOW STONE CEILING

BERRA

Basic shape of the stone triangular shape, therefore joints with good structural properties
arranged like lattice girders, therefore increased load-bearing capacity of the construction
low dead weight, therefore little iron required (round bar)
large cross-section of the cavities, therefore good soundproofing and heat retention, formation of condensation water impossible, first-class, pressure-resistant clay material
breakage during transportation excluded
easy assembly and many combination possibilities in use
utilized in our experimental building for the ceiling over all rooms on the ground floor, especially noteworthy the free span of the 6×6 m central room.

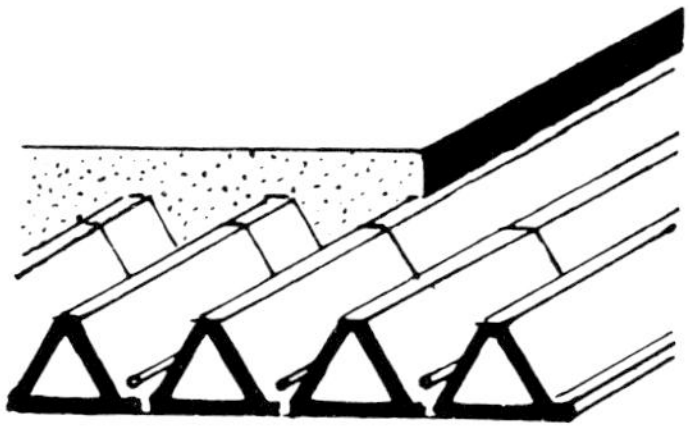

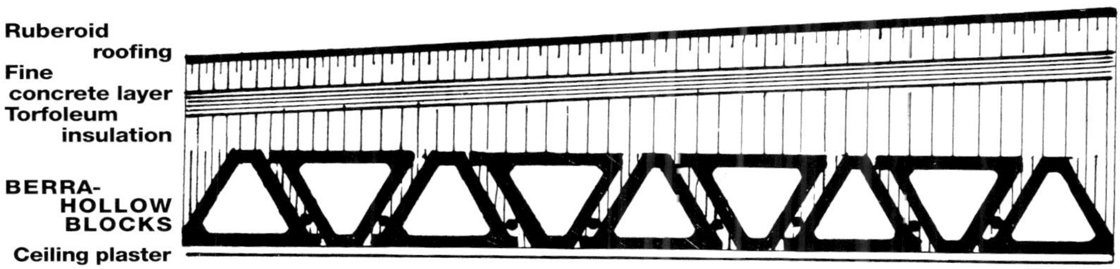

BERRA HOLLOW BLOCK CEILING:

BERKES & RÜCKER, WORMS AM RHEIN.
SUPPLY OF BERRA HOLLOW BLOCKS: BERRAVERTRIEBS-GES. M.B.H., NAUMBURG A.D.S.
EXECUTION BY A. &. K. HEURING, A.-G., MELLRICHSTADT (LOWER FRANCONIA)

Illustration above and page **30:** FITTING BERRA HOLLOW BLOCK ROOF

INSULATION

TORFOLEUM

COMPLETE INSULATION OF THE FLOORS • WALLS • CEILINGS

AGAINST **COLD** AND **HEAT** BY **TORFOLEUM LIGHTWEIGHT PANELS**

LIVING SPACES COOL IN SUMMER • WARM IN WINTER • HIGH INSULATION VALUE WITH MINIMUM WEIGHT PER VOLUME • REDUCTION OF WALL THICKNESSES • UNIQUE SAVINGS ON BRICKS, TRANSPORT COSTS, LABOR COSTS • PERMANENT SAVINGS ON HEATING MATERIAL

• IMPORTANT BUILDING MATERIAL •

TORFOLEUM INSULATION OF THE FLOOR UNDER THE SCREED

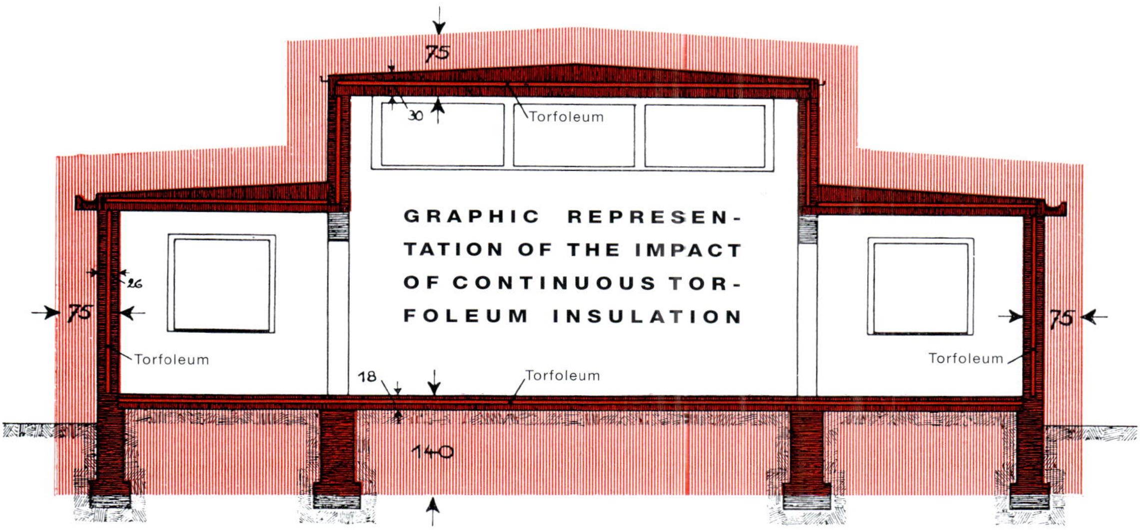

THE RED HATCHED AREA SHOWS THE REQUIRED FLOOR, WALL AND CEILING THICKNESS IN BRICK MASONRY TO ACHIEVE THE SAME INSULATING EFFECT WITHOUT TORFOLEUM

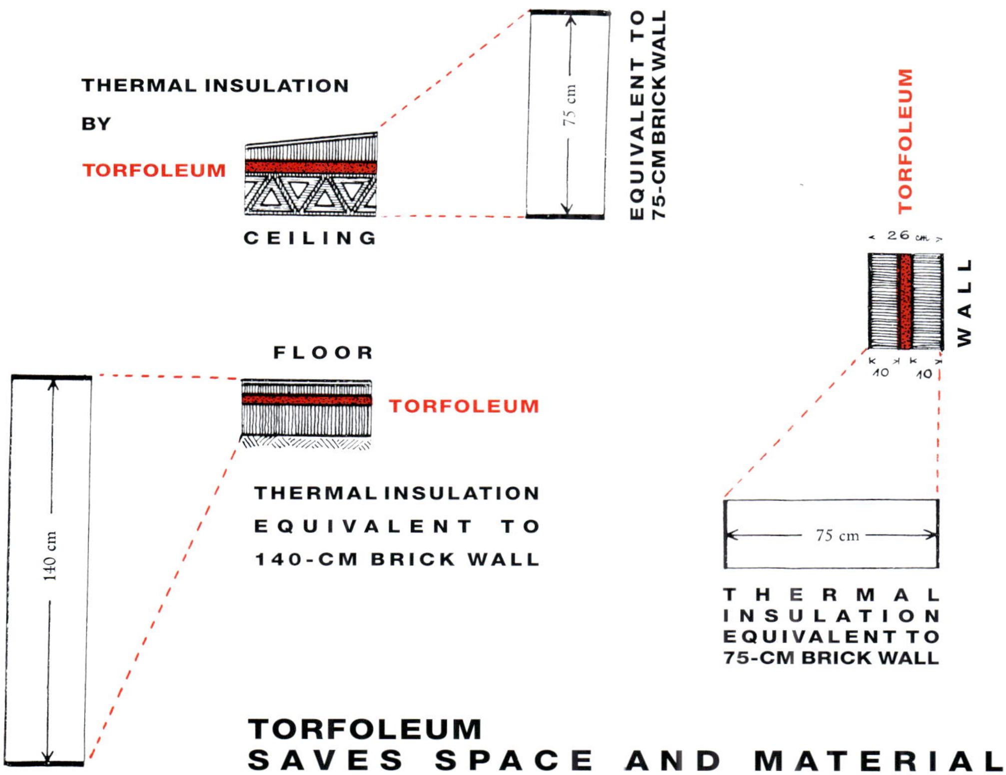

TORFOLEUM SAVES SPACE AND MATERIAL

34 INSTALLED TORFOLEUM INSULATION

SAVINGS
ATTAINED

25% CONSTRUCTION COSTS OF SURROUNDING WALLS AND ROOFS
27% COST OF CENTRAL HEATING SYSTEM (BOILER AND RADIATORS)
ANNUALLY: 82 CENTNER [8.2 TONS] FUEL

TORFOLEUM
PANELS SUPPLIED BY:
TORFOLEUM-WERKE EDUARD DYCKERHOFF
POGGENHAGEN 50 NEAR NEUSTADT AM RÜBENBERGE

APPLICATION OF THE TORFOLEUM PANELS TO THE ROOF SURFACES

ROOF COVERING

RUBEROID

Can be laid on any roof pitch
can be walked on
storm-proof
non-drip therefore always clean
no clogging of rain gutters
requires no maintenance painting
allows connections to walls, chimneys, sky-lights etc., therefore zinc edgings can be dispensed with

**RUBEROID A.-G.
HAMBURG**

paint can be applied on it
odorless and insensitive to acids, gases, fumes
protection against heat and cold, as can be insulated.

APPLYING THE RUBEROID COVERING TO THE ROOF

TERRANOVA
FINISHING RENDER

weather-resistant
indestructible
no need for paint

EXTERIOR FACADE PLASTER AND INTERIOR WALL PLASTER OF THE ENTRANCE VESTIBULE IN SILVER GREY TERRANOVA PLASTER

TERRANOVA-INDUSTRIE, FREIHUNG (UPPER PALATINATE)

FULGURIT
FULGURIT ASBESTOS SLATE PANELS

high flexural strength, tensile strength, compressive strength and high impact resistance, low specific weight, significant elasticity, good frost and weather resistance, perfectly impermeable to water, good fire resistance, low thermal conductivity, smooth even surfaces, easy to transport

STANDARDIZED CONSTRUCTION PIECES, READY TO USE FROM THE FACTORY, EASY ASSEMBLY, LABOR SAVING ON THE CONSTRUCTION SITE

FULGURITWERKE ADOLF OESTERHELD, EICHRIEDE NEAR WUNSTORF (HANOVER).

SUPPLY OF THE COVER PLATES FOR THE WINDOW SILLS IN FULGURIT-CEMENT-ASBESTOS SLATE

SYNTHETIC STONE

structurally sound building material
in a range of colors and grain sizes
can be produced anywhere, independent of the quarry in contrast to natural stone. Saving on transport costs

ENTRANCE STAIRS, CELLAR STAIRS, SLAB FLOORING ENTRYWAY, CEMENT SLAB FLOORING IN THE CELLAR ROOMS WITH WALL SKIRTING, GARDEN STEPS

SYNTHETIC STONE WORK: JOHANN HERMANN TREBITZ, JENA, KUNSTSTEIN- UND PLATTENFABRIK

B

FINISHING WORK

HB WROUGHT IRON WINDOWS DRGM

HERMANN BULNHEIM / BAUTZEN

SIDE SKYLIGHT WINDOWS OF THE CENTRAL LIVING AREA, THE SKYLIGHT ABOVE THE HALLWAY AND THE CELLAR LIGHT SHAFTS

Factory-made, ready-to-assemble standardized construction parts
Supporting structure, partly absorbs ceiling loads, window frames do not swell
large areas letting in light with low rung and frame thicknesses
Introduction to residential building also desired

38 JOINERY WORK WINDOWS

DESIGN: STATE BAUHAUS

WOODEN REVOLVING WINDOWS FOR THE LIVING SPACE

EXECUTION OF THE WOODEN FRAMES: **GLASERMEISTER MARTINI / WEIMAR**
REVOLVING WINDOW SPECIAL FITTING: **C. ARNOLDI / HAMBURG**
WINDOW HANDLES AND SASH LOCKS: **S. A. LOEVY / BERLIN**
REFLECTIVE GLAZING: **VEREIN DEUTSCHER SPIEGELGLAS-FABRIKEN / KÖLN AM RHEIN**

POLISHED PLATE GLASS

UTILIZATION: THE WHOLE LIVING SPACE AND BASEMENT WINDOWS, PARTLY IN FROSTED GLASS. ALL MIRRORS ON THE WALLS AND FURNITURE. GLASS PARTS OF THE BUILT-IN FURNITURE AND LIGHTING UNITS. WINDOW-SILLS, SKIRTING BOARDS, WALL COVERINGS IN KITCHENS AND BATHROOMS, WASHBASINS, ETC. IN WHITE, BLACK AND RED OPAQUE MIRROR GLASS

calm incident light, as the glass surfaces are completely flat, polished and parallel; the elegant glass material is only revealed through grinding and polishing (a crucial element in ensuring the building creates a clear exterior and interior impression)
pleasant appearance, as views outside are not distorted in contrast to ordinary, uneven window glass. Heat-retaining, therefore no need for double glazing
cozy and keeps out noise from the street due its thickness.
important building element, as it allows large undivided window openings not divided by rungs
durable, as 6–8 mm thick in contrast to 2–3 mm thick window glass
higher acquisition costs, but greater durability and resistance to gusts of wind, hailstorms and breakage hazards

See illustrations page 18, 38, 45 to 48, 50 to 51, 53, 55, 57, 60, 66 to 76

FOR ALL SUPPLIES:

VEREIN DEUTSCHER SPIEGELGLAS-FABRIKEN G. M. B. H., KÖLN AM RHEIN

VIA THE GLASS FOUNDERIES:

ALTWASSER IN SCHLESIEN
DEUTSCHE SPIEGELGLAS A.-G. FREDEN
WALDHOF NEAR MANNHEIM

40

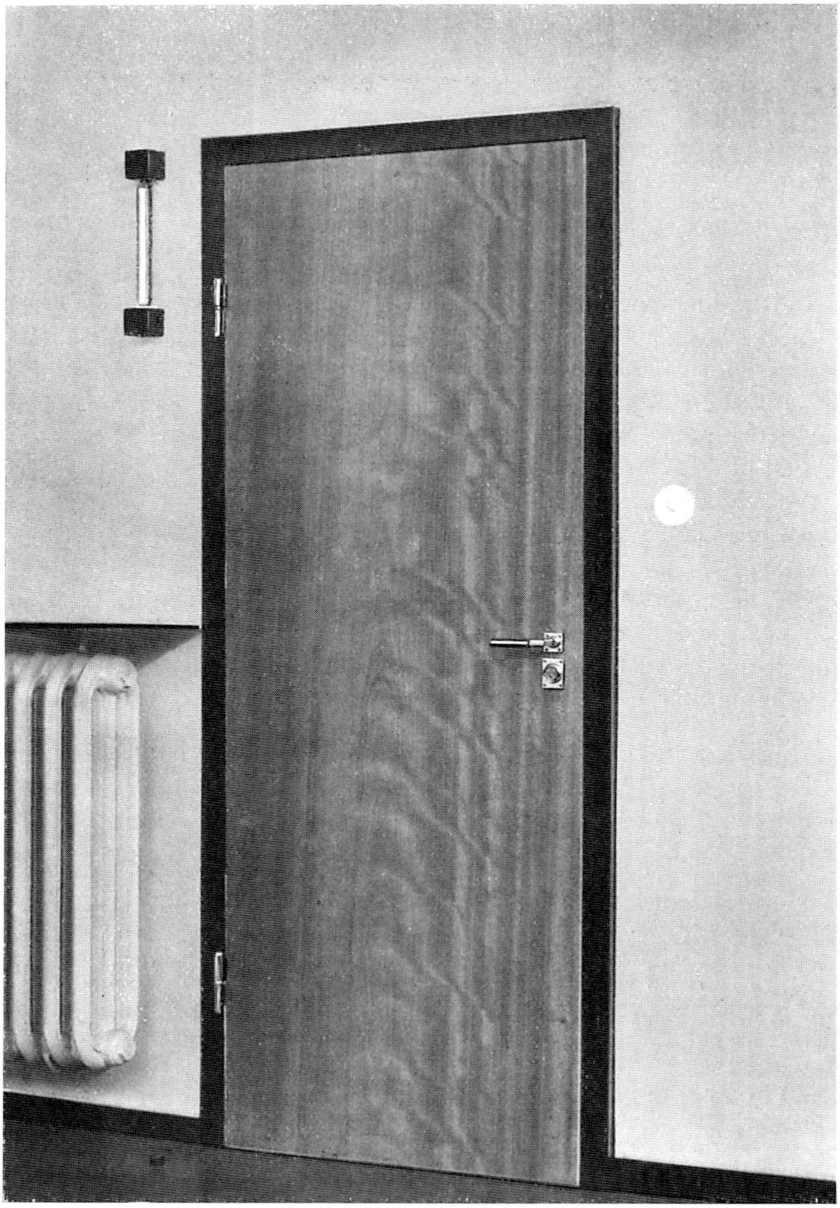

PLYWOOD DOOR IN THE LIVING ROOM

SKIRTING BOARDS: BLACK OPAQUE GLASS
LIGHTING UNIT: MIRRORED TUBE LAMP (BAUHAUS METAL WORKSHOP)

JOINERY WORK

DOORS

M. HARRAS G. M. B. H., BÖHLEN

PLYWOOD FACTORY
KOPTOXYL PANELS

large flush smooth surfaces without frames and in-fill
no warping
no working of the wood
mass produced, therefore spare construction components are available off the shelf

See illustration on page 40

DOOR HANDLE
NICKEL-PLATED
CAST BRONZE

SUPPLY OF METAL FITTINGS: S.A. LOEVY, BERLIN N 4

B. K. S. SECURITY CYLINDER LOCK FROM: W. LÖSCH, WEIMAR

DOOR FRAMES MANNSTAEDT

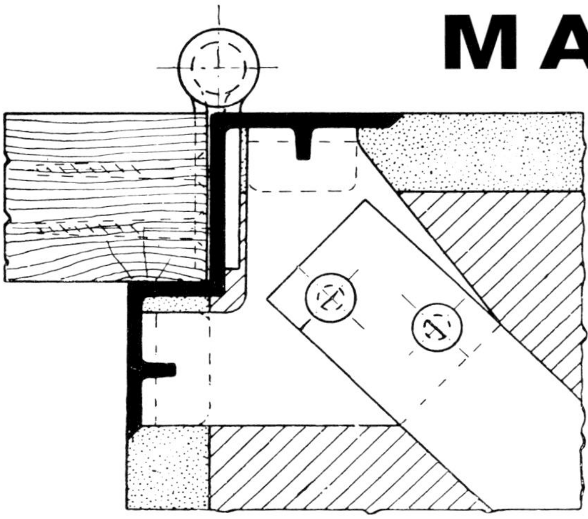

RHEINISCH-WESTFÄLISCHE KLÖCKNER-WERKE A.-G. MANNSTAEDTWERKE UNIT TROISDORF NEAR COLOGNE

flush, joint-free connection to the plaster
no crumbling of the plaster
riveting on the back of the stone anchors
no riveting spots on the construction sides
connection of the frame corners by electric welding, therefore inseparable joining of frame parts to form a whole
thorough, convenient cleaning, as there are no moldings
unlimited durability, therefore no need for repairs

MASS PRODUCED; READY-TO-ASSEMBLE STANDARDIZED CONSTRUCTION PARTS

MANNSTAEDT DOOR FRAMES

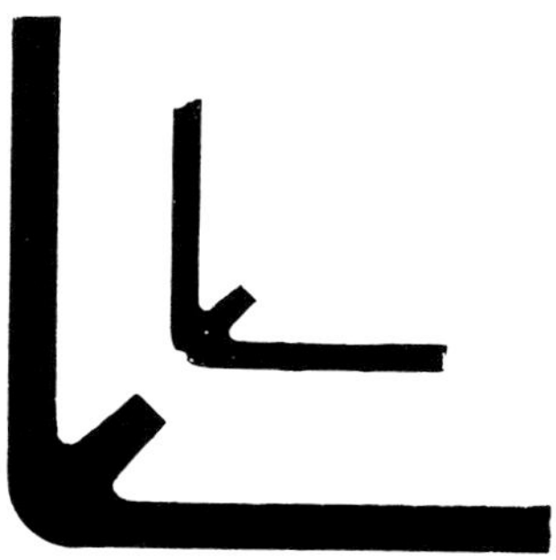

CORNER PROTECTORS

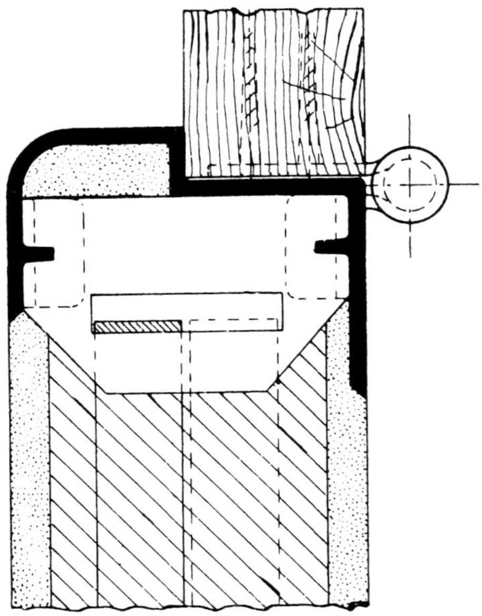

MANNSTAEDT PATENTED DOOR FRAMES AND CORNER PROTECTORS IN KITCHEN, BATHROOM, TOILET

FLOORS

RUBBER FLOOR COVERING

IN DINING ROOM AND BATHROOM

noise-free supple walking surface
excellent cleanliness
washable
does not alter in response to temperature influences
completely dyed throughout
almost permanently durable industrial product
provides insulation against heat and cold
ideal floor covering

HARBURGER
GUMMIWAREN-FABRIK
PHÖNIX A.-G.
HARBURG A.E.

See illustration p. 70 and 71

TRIOLIN

FLOORING IN THE LIVING SPACE, KITCHEN AND TOILET EXCEPT FOR DINING ROOM AND BATHROOM

Industrial product, inexpensive and durable
insulates against heat and cold
excellent cleanliness
easy floor cleaning, since jointless
does not alter with changing temperatures
soft comfortable walking surface

SOLD BY

SALES OFFICE OF THE KÖLN-ROTTWEIL-AKT.-GES. AND RHEINISCH-WESTF. SPRENG-STOFFABRIK BERLIN NW 40 THROUGH LEIPZIG BRANCH

See illustration page 67, 68

C
INSTALLATION WORKS

1. SANITARY INSTALLATION:
   WATER, GAS AND ENERGY SUPPLY FOR CONSTRUCTION OF THE BATHROOM, TOILETS, KITCHEN AND LAUNDRY ROOM
2. THERMAL INSTALLATION:
   CENTRAL HEATING SYSTEM, GAS AND ELECTRIC COOKING SYSTEM
3. ELECTRICAL INSTALLATION:
   LIGHT, BELL AND TELEPHONE SYSTEM

1. SANITARY INSTALLATION

TRITON WERKE A.-G. HAMBURG

SUPPLY OF FIXTURES FOR BATHROOMS, TOILETS AND KITCHEN, (BATHTUBS, WASHBASINS, SINKS)

all parts washable smooth,
jointless, concise use-oriented design of the bathroom equipment and nickel-plated fittings
white, acid-resistant, almost indestructible material (fire clay)
no surfaces on which dust can settle, no moldings
significantly facilitates the housewife's work in tackling everyday chores
hygienic bathrooms and washing facilities

BUILT-IN BATHTUB AND GAS BOILER IN THE BATHROOM

ALABASTER GLASS WALL AND BATHTUB CLADDING MADE BY DEUTSCHE SPIEGELGLAS-A.-G.
FREDEN AN DER LEINE

46

WASHBASIN IN THE CHILDREN'S ROOM

ALABASTER GLASS DESIGN FROM DEUTSCHER SPIEGELGLAS-A.-G. FREDEN AN DER LEINE.
POLISHED PLATE GLASS: VEREIN DEUTSCHER SPIEGELGLASFABRIKEN G.M.B.H., KÖLN AM RHEIN

TRITON
WERKE
HAMBURG

WASHBASIN IN THE BATHROOM

CLADDING OF ALL WALL SURFACES WITH ALABASTER GLASS FROM DEUTSCHER SPIEGEL-GLAS-A.-G. FREDEN AN DER LEINE. POLISHED PLATE GLASS: VEREIN DEUTSCHER SPIEGEL-GLASFABRIKEN G.M.B.H., KÖLN AM RHEIN

TRITON WERKE HAMBURG

48 TRITON WERKE HAMBURG

WALL AND CEILING CLADDING: WHITE OPAQUE GLASS.
DEUTSCHER SPIEGELGLAS-A.-G., FREDEN AN DER LEINE

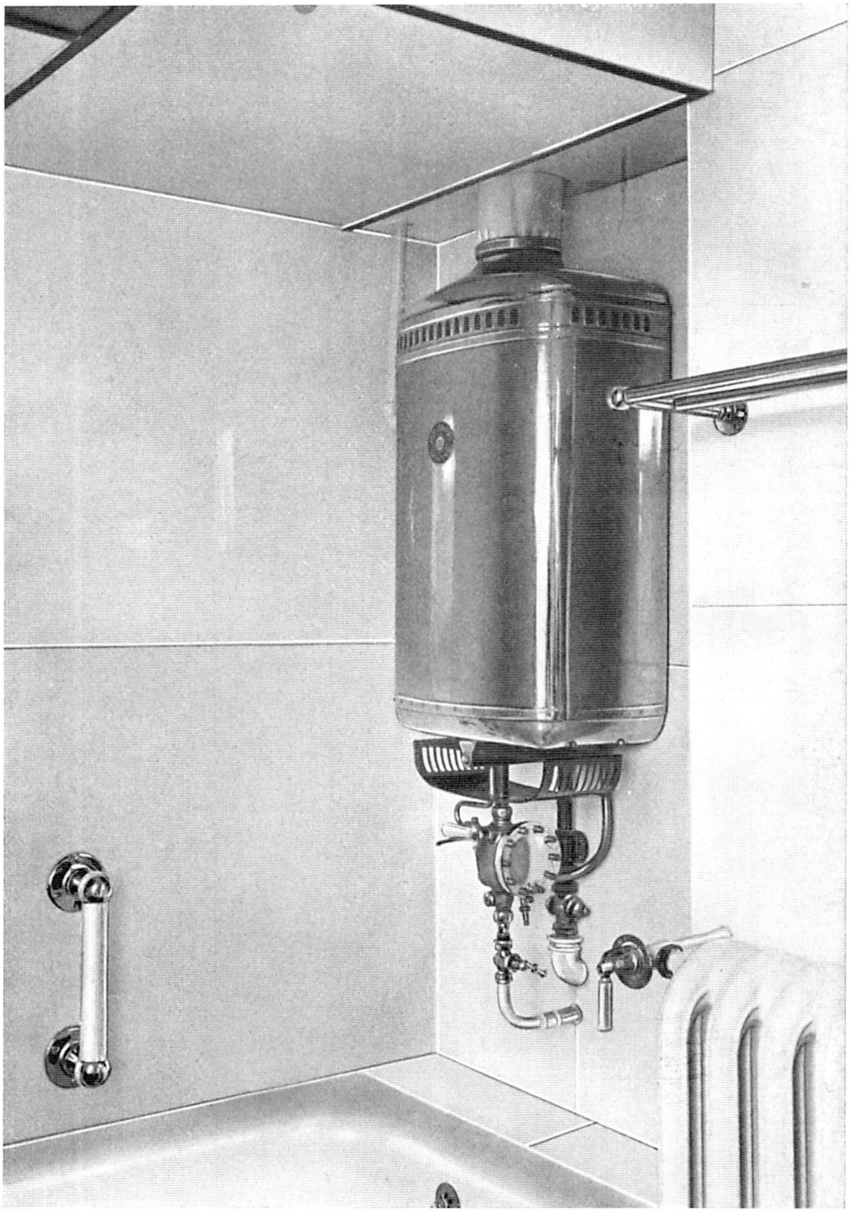

JUNKERS & CO. DESSAU

GAS BOILER IN THE BATHROOM

KITCHEN | BATH-ROOM

HOT WATER SUPPLY

JUNKERS & CO.
DESSAU

KITCHEN:
PROFESSOR JUNKER'S FAST WATER HEATER
BATHROOM:
PROFESSOR JUNKER'S COPPER BATHROOM BOILER
(NICKEL-PLATED)

Extremely low, economical consumption of gas
smooth organic design
saves time and labor for the housewife
takes up little space
See illustration page 48, 50

KITCHEN STOVE

IMPERIAL

GAS ROASTING AND GRILLING STOVE DOUBLE OVEN D. R. P. AND D. R. G. M.

smooth, washable form
ease of use for the housewife
no fire lighting
no wood or coal transport needed
optimum utilization of heating material, as it can be easily regulated and switched off
See illustration on page 53

INDUSTRIEWERKE VOGEL, KOMMANDITGESELL-SCHAFT AUF AKTIEN, BÜNDE IN WESTPHALIA

TRITON
WERKE
HAMBURG

WALL CLADDING: WHITE OPAQUE GLASS
DEUTSCHER SPIEGELGLAS-A.-G., FREDEN AN DER LEINE

JUNKERS
& CO.
DESSAU

KITCHEN DRAINBOARD SINK WITH FAST WATER HEATER

TRITON WERKE HAMBURG 51

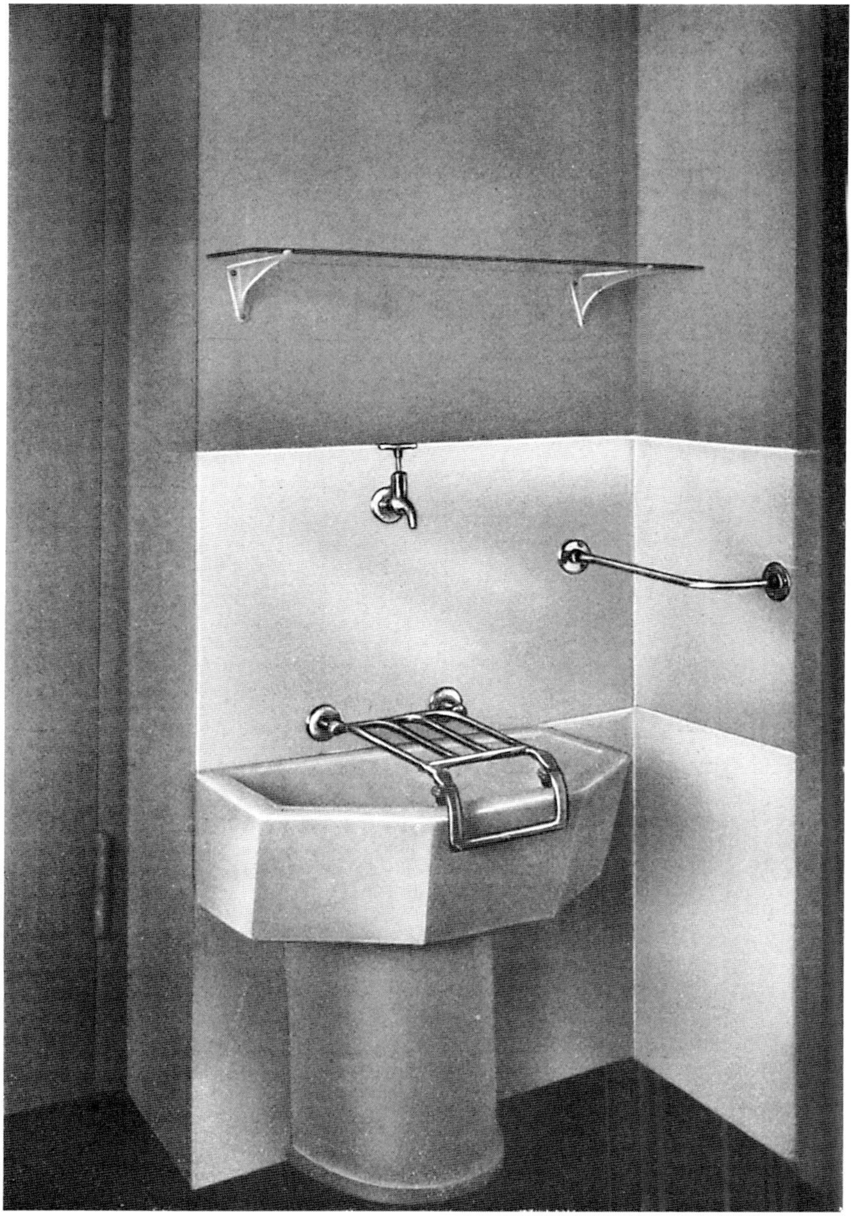

LARGE WHITE OPAQUE GLASS WALL CLADDING
DEUTSCHER SPIEGELGLAS-A.-G., FREDEN AN DER LEINE

KITCHEN **UTILITY SINK**

KITCHEN **DRAINBOARD SINK, CUPBOARD, WORK TABLE**

DESIGN: B. OTTE AND E. GEBHARDT, STATE BAUHAUS
CONTAINERS. MODEL: T. BOGLER, STATE BAUHAUS; FACTORY PRODUCTION BY STEINGUTFABRIKEN
VELTEN VORDAMM G.M.B.H., VELTEN-BERLIN
GLASS COOK AND BAKEWARE. DURAXGLAS, SCHOTT & GEN., GLASWERKE JENA

KITCHEN

PARTIAL VIEW WITH GAS STOVE

IMPERIAL KITCHEN STOVE WITH ADJOINING WORK TABLE FLUSH
WALL CLADDING: WHITE OPAQUE GLASS
SPICE JARS. DESIGN: T. BOGLER, CERAMIC WORKSHOP OF THE STATE BAUHAUS; FACTORY PRODUCTION BY
STEINGUTFABRIKEN VELTEN VORDAMM G.M.B.H.

COLORED OPAQUE GLASS

LINING OF BATHROOM WALLS AND NICHES, WALL COVERING IN KITCHEN, RADIATOR COVER PANELS, WINDOW SILLS, SKIRTING BOARDS, WASHBASIN TOPS AND TABLE TOPS

OPAQUE GLASS is a premium building material with particularly favorable properties:

OPAQUE GLASS

is, unlike marble, not porous; opaque glass can be cut to every shape and worked very easily

OPAQUE GLASS

has a completely even surface, no nail holes, etc., it does not weather and is far superior to fire-polished colored glass

OPAQUE GLASS

does not refract the light and thus provides excellent reflection. Opaque glass is also acid-resistant and does not discolor as a result of acids, alkalis or other chemicals, does not absorb oil and therefore always retains its full beauty

OPAQUE GLASS

is suitable for wall coverings on exterior surfaces as well as for interior room design with unlimited application possibilities

Colors: white, black, red and red-veined, also in other colors

Available in sizes up to 350 cm lateral length, in thicknesses from 6 to 32 mm

See page 38, 45 to 48, 50 to 53, 55, 57, 60, 66 to 76

**DEUTSCHE SPIEGELGLAS-A.-G.
FREDEN AN DER LEINE**

WINDOWS WITH SUNBLINDS LOWERED

SUNBLIND: C. ARNOLDI, HAMBURG, RATHAUSSTRASSE 5. WINDOW SILL: OPAQUE GLASS

2. THERMAL INSTALLATION

CENTRAL HEATING SYSTEM JOHANNES HAAG / BERLIN-WEIMAR

FABRIK FÜR ZENTRALHEIZUNGEN

Advantages of central heating systems:

concentration of fuel and boiler in one place
no need to move fuel around inside the house
convenient operation and regulation, labor saving
Good fuel utilization
even heating of the whole house
Compact form of radiators
no dust deposits

RADIATORS: BERLIN-BURGER EISENWERK A.-G., BERLIN W 8

See page 57

RADIATORS WITH OPAQUE GLASS PANELS

RADIATORS: BERLIN-BURGER EISENWERK

3.

E L E C T R I C A L I N S T A L L A T I O N

Electricity is the most important tool to mechanize work – saving time, energy and space. Industrially manufactured products for the electrical industry have made clear progress towards the formation of standard typologies.
Standardized installation parts offer all the advantages of ease in obtaining spare parts, interchangeability of parts, availability of parts to any installer.

LIGHTING SYSTEM

A E G

ALLGEMEINE ELEKTRIZITÄTSGESELLSCHAFT

B E R L I N

IN CONNECTION WITH THE

O S R A M

GESELLSCHAFT

B E R L I N

In arranging light sources and distributing luminous intensities and effects, efforts have been made to make the artificial lighting an organic component of the spatial effect produced in each instance.

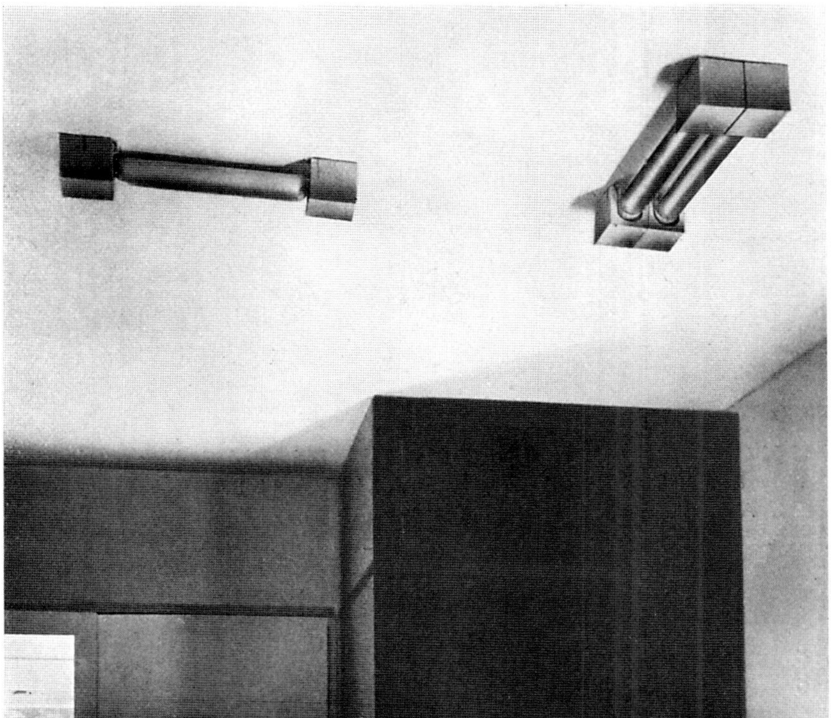

TUBULAR LIGHTING FIXTURE
BY OSRAMGESELLSCHAFT BERLIN

LIGHTING IN THE GENTLEMAN'S ROOM
BAUHAUS METAL WORKSHOP

60

LIGHTING FIXTURES IN THE DINING ROOM
METAL WORKSHOP OF THE BAUHAUS
CEILING PANEL COATED, LOWER
PANEL MATT POLISHED PLATE GLASS

LIGHTING FIXTURES IN THE GUEST ROOM AND IN THE TOILET
PORCELAIN FITTINGS IN THE CEILING FLUSH-FITTED
J. KARL, ELEKTROTECHNISCHE FABRIK, OBERWEIMAR

62 CONTROL PANEL

WESTFÄLISCH-ANHALTISCHE SPRENG-STOFF-AKTIENGESELLSCHAFT BERLIN METER BOARD “WASAG”

new artificial material (Wasagit pressed material)
high insulating capacity, high mechanical strength
completely non-hygroscopic
possibility of replacing fuse elements and installation of new circuits without removing the board from the wall

BELL LINE TELE-PHONE SYSTEM

THÜRINGISCHE TELEPHON-GESELLSCHAFT ERFURT

HOME LAUNDRY EQUIPMENT

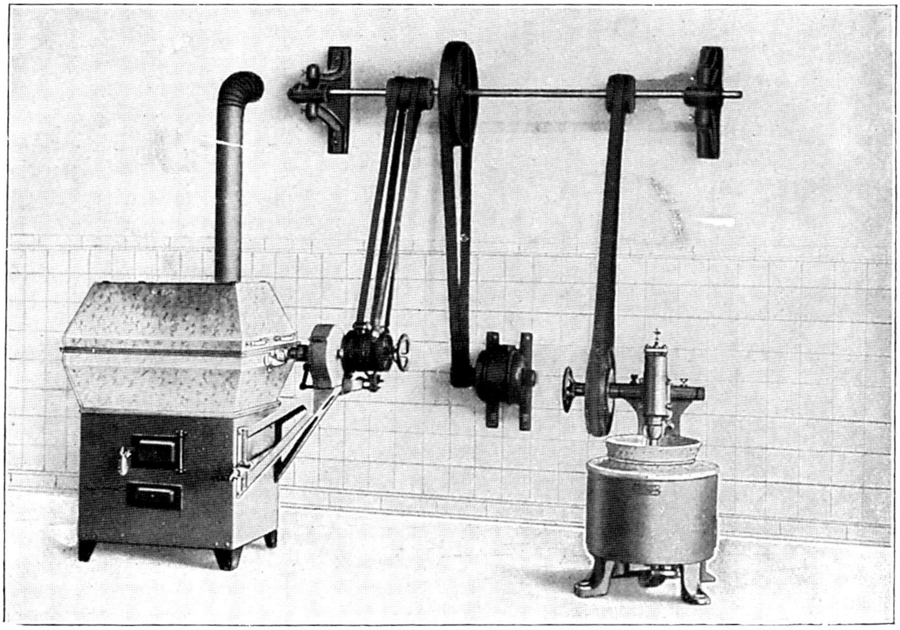

J. A. JOHN, AKTIENGESELLSCHAFT
ERFURT - ILVERSGEHOFEN
HOME LAUNDRY EQUIPMENT WITH
GAS HEATING AND ELECTRIC DRIVE

Mechanization of the bulk of the work
75 % savings in heating and detergents, in time and personnel, and is gentle on the laundry

OVERALL VIEW FROM THE SOUTH-WEST

D
INTERIOR DESIGN

BAUHAUS WORKSHOPS

ALL THE WORKSHOPS WERE INVOLVED IN SETTING UP THE EXPERIMENTAL HOUSE:

STONE SCULPTURE

JOS. HARTWIG	HOUSE MODEL

CARPENTRY

MARCEL BREUER	LIVING ROOM AND LADY'S ROOM
ALMA BUSCHER AND ERICH BRENDEL	CHILDREN'S ROOM
ERICH DIECKMANN	DINING AND GENTLEMAN'S ROOM
BENITA OTTE AND ERNST GEBHARDT	KITCHEN

METAL WORKSHOP

ALMA BUSCHER	LIGHTING IN CHILDREN'S ROOM
C. J. JUCKER	DESK LAMPS
JULIUS PAP	FLOOR LAMPS IN LIVING ROOM

WALL PAINTING

ALFRED ARNDT AND JOSEPH MALTAN	INTERIOR PAINTING

WEAVING WORKSHOP

LIS DEINHARDT	RUG IN GENTLEMAN'S ROOM
MARTHA ERPS	RUG IN LIVING ROOM
BENITA OTTE	RUG IN CHILDREN'S ROOM
AGNES ROGHÉ	RUG IN LADY'S ROOM
GUNTA STÖLZL	RUG IN LIVING ROOM NICHE

CERAMIC WORKSHOP

THEO BOGLER AND OTTO LINDIG	CERAMIC CONTAINERS

66

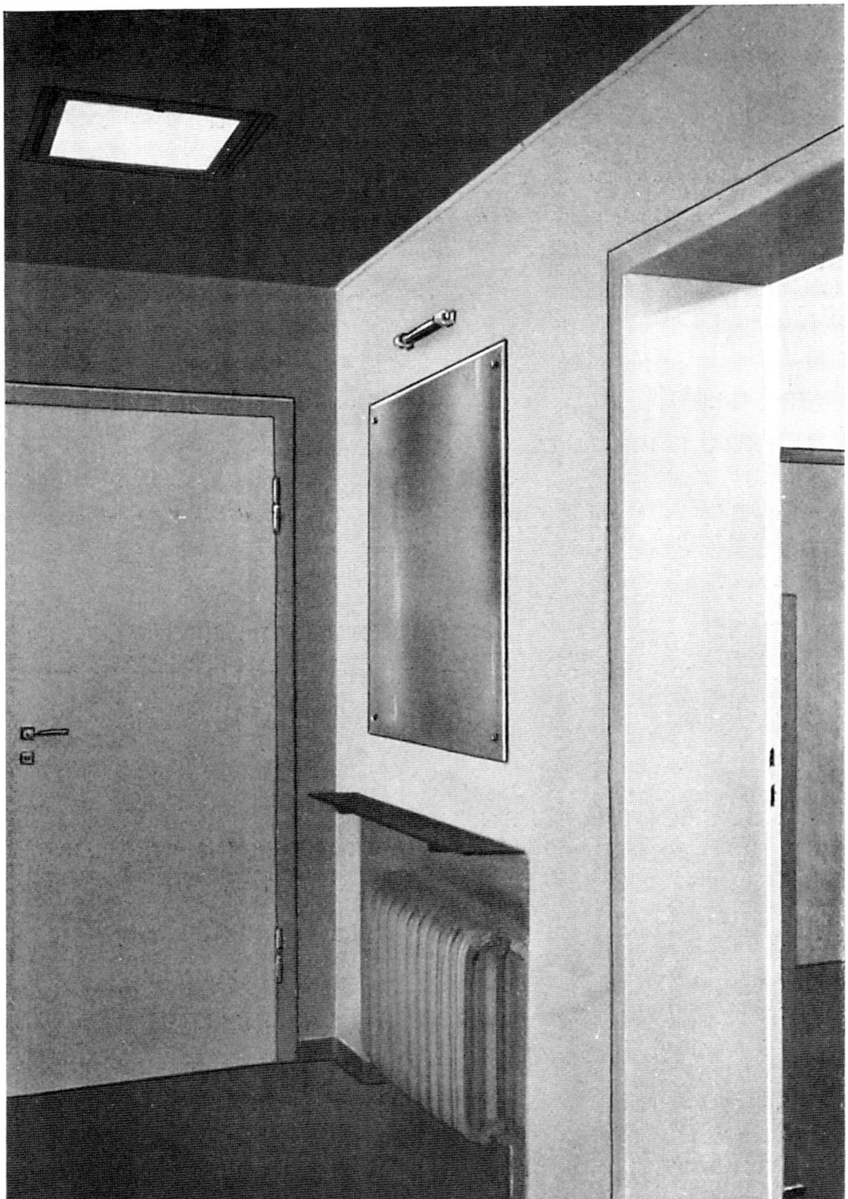

VESTIBULE

RADIATORS WITH OPAQUE GLASS PLATE AND WARDROBE MIRROR: DEUTSCHE SPIEGELGLAS-A.-G., FREDEN A. D. LEINE. MANNSTAEDT DOOR FRAMES. SKYLIGHT: WROUGHT-IRON HB-WINDOW

DESK. DESIGN: M. BREUER. EXECUTION: STATE BAUHAUS. SKYLIGHT: WROUGHT-IRON HB-WINDOW. TRIOLIN FLOORING

LIVING ROOM WITH WORK NICHE

CABINET IN THE LIVING ROOM

CABINET. DESIGN: M. BREUER. GREY MATT MAPLE, RED MATT PADUK, MATT HUNGARIAN ASH, BLACK POLISHED PEARWOOD, POLISHED NICKEL FITTINGS. OPAQUE GLASS PLATE ABOVE THE RADIATOR. TRIOLIN FLOORING.

FURNITURE. DESIGN: M. BREUER. EXECUTION: STATE BAUHAUS. RUG. DESIGN AND EXECUTION: M. ERPS. WEAVING: STATE BAUHAUS. BLACK OPAQUE GLASS PLATE ABOVE RADIATOR

VIEW INTO THE LIVING ROOM FROM THE DINING ROOM

70

DESIGN: E. DIECKMANN. EXECUTION: STATE BAUHAUS. FURNITURE: BLACK MATT OAK. CHAIRS WITH NATURAL-COLORED RUSHES. TABLETOP: GREY BIRD'SEYE MAPLE, WITH POLISHED PLATE GLASS TOP. RED-BLUE-WHITE RUBBER FLOORING

DINING ROOM

DINING ROOM

DESIGN: E. DIECKMANN, EXECUTION: STATE BAUHAUS. FURNITURE: OAK, BLACK, MATT. CHAIRS WITH NATURAL-COLORED RUSHES. TABLETOP: GRAY BIRD'S EYE MAPLE, WITH POLISHED PLATE GLASS TOP. RUBBER FLOORING

GENTLEMAN'S ROOM

DESIGN: E. DIECKMANN. EXECUTION: STATE BAUHAUS. FURNITURE: MATT (RED) PADUK AND MATT (BLACK) OAK. BEDSIDE RUG: L. DEINHARDT. WEAVING: STATE BAUHAUS. LIGHTING: MOHOLY-NAGY. BAUHAUS METAL WORKSHOP (SEE PAGE 59).

DESIGN: E. DIECKMANN. EXECUTION: STATE BAUHAUS. FURNITURE: MATT (RED) PADUK AND MATT (BLACK) OAK. LIGHTING: BAUHAUS METAL WORKSHOP

GENTLEMAN'S ROOM VIEW INTO THE BATHROOM

74

DESIGN: A. BUSCHER AND E. BRENDEL. EXECUTION: STATE BAUHAUS. WALL SURFACES: COLORFUL WOOD PANELS THAT CAN BE USED FOR WRITING AND MATHEMATICS. MULTI-COLORED PLAY BLOCKS TO BUILD WITH AND AS SEATS FOR THE CHILDREN. WALL CUPBOARD FOR TOYS, CAN BE USED AS A PUPPET THEATER. LIGHTING FIXTURE: CIRCULAR MATT PLATE GLASS

CHILDREN'S ROOM WITH A VIEW THROUGH THE DINING ROOM INTO THE KITCHEN

LADY'S ROOM

DESIGN: M. BREUER. EXECUTION: STATE BAUHAUS. FURNITURE: LEMONWOOD, WALNUT, RUG DESIGN AND EXECUTION: A. ROGHÉ. WEAVING: STATE BAUHAUS

DESIGN AND EXECUTION: M. BREUER, STATE BAUHAUS. LEMONWOOD AND WALNUT WOOD. FITTINGS: POLISHED NICKEL. WITH ADJUSTABLE MIRRORS

LADY'S DRESSING TABLE

GENERAL VIEW WITH GARDEN ENTRANCE GATE

RUDOLF BASCHANDT: Garden plan and garden gate.

GUSTAV ARENDT & SOHN, WEIMAR: Garden fencing using patented wire fence connections from Nord-Drahtwerke Rostock provided via representative Richard Treisse, Coburg.

CONRAD GRAMM, TREE NURSERIES, WEIMAR: Garden.

78 MISCELLANEOUS

THE FOLLOWING WERE INVOLVED IN THE INTERIOR DESIGN OF THE HOUSE:

G. & H. SCHÜTZE, MASTER CARPENTER TO THE COURT, BERLIN S, URBANSTRASSE 64: Supply of the built-in closets and doors in the lady's bedroom.

A. FINN, MASTER CARPENTER, WEIMAR: Door frames and cladding.

PAUL AND ERNST MEYER, MASTER LOCKSMITHS, WEIMAR: Work on locks and fittings.

WILHELM LÖSCH, WEIMAR: Supplier for locks and fittings.

RUDOLF HEINZE, WEIMAR: Terranova supplier.

KARL SCHMIDT, ENGINEER, WEIMAR: Execution of sanitary installation.

HERMANN BACHMANN, WEIMAR: Execution of electrotechnical installation.

SANTO VACUUM CLEANER VAMPYR, BERLIN.

ERNST KRAUS, WEIMAR: assembly of glass claddings, plate and opaque glass.

GUSTAV ARENDT & SOHN, WEIMAR: Patented spring mattresses for beds in lady's, gentleman's and children's rooms.

STEINGUTFABRIKEN VELTEN VORDAMM G. M. B. H., VELTEN NEAR BERLIN: Supplier of stoneware tableware based on Bauhaus models.

GLASWERKE SCHOTT & GEN., JENA: Supplier of glassware for the kitchen (Durax glass baking utensils).

ALBERT LANGEN VERLAG MÜNCHEN
PUBLISHES, AS A SERIES, THE

BAUHAUSBÜCHER

Editors: GROPIUS and MOHOLY-NAGY

THE FIRST SERIES COMPRISES 8 VOLUMES

1 INTERNATIONALE ARCHITEKTUR by WALTER GROPIUS
2 PÄDAGOGISCHES SKIZZENBUCH by PAUL KLEE
3 EIN VERSUCHSHAUS DES BAUHAUSES
4 DIE BÜHNE IM BAUHAUS
5 NEUE GESTALTUNG by PIET MONDRIAN (Holland)
6 GRUNDBEGRIFFE DER NEUEN KUNST by THEO VAN DOESBURG (Holland)
7 NEUE ARBEITEN DER BAUHAUSWERKSTÄTTEN
8 MALEREI, PHOTOGRAPHIE, FILM by L. MOHOLY-NAGY

FURTHER PLANNED VOLUMES:
KLEINWOHNUNGEN by BAUHAUS ARCHITECTURE DEPARTMENT
MERZ-BUCH by KURT SCHWITTERS
BILDERMAGAZIN DER ZEIT by OSKAR SCHLEMMER
SCHÖPFERISCHE MUSIKERZIEHUNG by HEINRICH JACOBY
AMERIKA? – EUROPA? by GEORG MUCHE
DIE ARBEIT DER STIJL-GRUPPE by THEO VAN DOESBURG
KONSTRUKTIVE BIOLOGIE by MARTIN SCHÄFER
DIE HOLLÄNDISCHE ARCHITEKTUR by J. J. P. OUD (Holland)
FUTURISMUS by F. T. MARINETTI and E. PRAMPOLINI (Italy)
DIE ARBEIT DER MA-GRUPPE by L. KASSÁK and E. KÁLLAI (Hungary)
PLASTIK DER GESTALTUNGEN by M. BURCHARTZ
PUNKT, LINIE, FLÄCHE by WASSILY KANDINSKY
RUSSLAND by ADOLF BEHNE
REKLAME UND TYPOGRAPHIE
NEUE ARCHITEKTURDARSTELLUNG by WALTER GROPIUS
BILDNERISCHE MECHANIK by PAUL KLEE
WERKARBEIT DER GESTALTUNGEN by L. MOHOLY-NAGY
ARCHITEKTUR, MALEREI, PLASTIK from the BAUHAUS WORKSHOPS
DIE NEUEN MATERIALIEN by ADOLF MEYER
ARCHITEKTUR by LE CORBUSIER-SAUGNIER (France)
BILDERMAGAZIN DER ZEIT II by JOOST SCHMIDT
VIOLETT (BÜHNENSTÜCK MIT EINLEITUNG UND SZENERIE) by KANDINSKY

Each volume contains circa **16** to **32** pages of text and **32** to **96** full-page illustrations or **48** to **60** pages of text ● Format **18 × 23** cm ●